To Purify the Words of the Tribe

To Purify the Words of the Tribe

The Major Verse Poems
of
Stéphane Mallarmé

With

UN COUP DE DÉS
JAMAIS N'ABOLIRA
LE HASARD

Translation from the French
by
Daisy Aldan
With expositions

Sky Blue Press

Huntington Woods, MI

Mallarmé, Stéphane.
    To Purify the Words of the Tribe.
    ISBN 0-9652364-3-9
    LCCN 98-61790

Acknowledgments

Thanks to Yvette Ripplinger for invaluable suggestions and to Terry Hulse for her tireless efforts in typing the original manuscript. Thanks to Lynn Sands Herron for her help in proofing.

Foreword

The majesty of Stéphane Mallarmé's poetry resides not alone in the lofty ideas and profound and poignant strivings, but in the form, the verse and sound structures which, when noted, contain the attributes which can thrill a lover of the art of poetry. Not one sound or syllable is superfluous. Each poem moves into deep seas of multiplicity of meaning and tone.

Having found no translations presently existing which seem consistently to grasp the experience of this profound individual, I have taken up the challenge in an attempt to bring the translation into English a step further. Because of the nature of the originals in which sound becomes essential to the total experience, the translations must serve only as keys, and must avoid that fallacy which attempts to recreate the rhyme schemes. However, surpassing literalness, they yet must themselves be poetry, while not as versions deviating from the originals.

I hope that through some singular grace, and through love of the work, to have reached into the ineffable which Mallarmé explored and from where inspiration has favored me, and thereby to assist readers in truly experiencing the poems.

—*Daisy Aldan*

Introduction

On March 18, 1842, at 12 rue Laferrière in Paris, Stéphane Mallarmé was born. Fifty-six years later, on September 9, 1898, he died in Valvins, breathless, strangled by cancer of the larynx brought about, no doubt, through his habit since youth of smoking his beloved pipe. It is ironic that such a death should have befallen him, for during his prolific yet short lifetime, he suffered from bouts of an unexplained malady of impotence and sterility, during which time his imaginative, inspiring genius seemed to desert him. He referred to it as "impuissance," and describes this state in a letter to his friend Henri Cazalis in 1862 when he wrote:

"Emmanuel [des Essarts] has perhaps spoken to you about a curious sterility with which Spring has imbued me. After three months of impotence, I have finally rid myself of it and my first sonnet is consecrated to describing it—that is, to cursing it."

The sonnet referred to is "Renouveau":

Sadly, the sickly Spring has banished
Winter, season of placid art, the lucid Winter,
And in my being, where my dismal blood presides
Impotence stretches like a slow yawn....

In March 1864, Mallarmé wrote to Cazalis in connection with his renowned poem, "L'Azur":

"It has given me infinite difficulty, aside from the fact that before taking pen in hand to master a moment of perfect lucidity, I had to overcome my nerve-wracking impotence...."

In his struggle to combat this state and to express it in words, he fashioned some of his most exquisite poems. The sterility becomes, finally, a universal symbol, surpassing the personal confessional.

Another significant but related theme was the agony experienced from the rejection by his contemporaries. Even his closest friends—poets—criticized his "obscurity," comprehending neither his lofty vision nor his aesthetic. Mallarmé's poems are never "obscure"; they are hermetic.

In a letter to Cazalis, he stated that he was attempting to paint "non la chose mais l'effet qu'elle produit" (not the thing but the effect which it produces).

In an interview conducted by Jules Huret for the periodical *Réponses à des Enquêtes,* Mallarmé stated:

> "To name an object is to suppress three fourths of the pleasure of the poem which is made to be divined bit by bit: To *suggest,* there's the dream. It's the perfect usage of the mystery which constitutes the symbols: To evoke, bit by bit, an object in order to convey a condition of soul, or inversely, to choose an object and to abstract from it a condition of soul by a series of abstractions."

The readers of his time were not equipped to fathom his concepts nor his references. His conviction was that the Poet (with a capital 'P') had a mandate never to debase his ideal in order to make his work comprehensible to the "mass," but instead to lift his readers to an enlarged vision, thereby raising consciousness. He longed for a reader who would make the same effort of creative cognition in the reading of the work as he had made in its realization. Thereby the reader would create himself as the poet does in the process of creation. Once he stated that it would be sufficient if there were one ideal reader, even if that reader were himself.

In spite of that lofty statement, he suffered profoundly from the isolation, and out of that agony emerged some of his major symbols and the pearls which that agony fashioned as his poems.

"Toast Funèbre," written as a dedication for the death of Théophile Gautier, eloquently expresses his convictions in symbols which were to recur in ever new contexts.

He refers to the uncomprehending as:

> "This haggard crowd! which proclaims: We are/ The pitiful opacity of our future spectres."

Is he perhaps referring to the *Book of Revelation,* which depicts a distant future when those bogged down in materialism will be cast out?

Yet, among the mourners, stands:

> "One of those passersby, proud, blind and mute,"/who "....might transform himself/ into the virgin hero of the posthumous hope."

The Poet's "œuvre" will spark that one to creativity, and that is enough to carry forth the evolution of consciousness. That "passerby" was present through destiny. (Mallarmé once referred to Rimbaud as "that considerable passerby.") He is the progeny of the creative genius, "proud," whose initial blindness and muteness will be awakened to clarity and lucidity through the work of the Master, as the blind man and the cripple were healed by the Word of the Christ. Thereby, he becomes the "virgin hero," transformed by the creative Word of the Master Poet, now deceased, who named for humanity its experience.

The "calm disaster" is a symbol Mallarmé used to refer to the descent to earth of the poetic genius who was like a meteorite (as Poe had been), who was sent to "purify the words of the tribe."

He goes on to say of the deceased Master Poet:

"Splendid eternal genius has no shade. I....wish to see/ For him who vanished yesterday, in the ideal/ Duty assigned to us by the gardens of this star,/ Survive in honor of the calm disaster/ A solemn agitation in the air/ Of words, intoxicating crimson and great clear chalice,/ Which rain and diamond, the translucent gaze/ Fixed on these flowers, not one of which fades,/ Isolates within the hour and the daylight glow!"

The "solemn agitation in the air" may be encountered frequently in Mallarmé's poems. It is the "wingbeat," the "fan-wing," which denotes the moment of illumination and inspiration which precedes creation. The "crimson and great clear chalice" echoes the Grail Cup with the blood of the Christ, "intoxicating" in the sense of life-enhancing spiritual nourishment. The "diamond" represents the ultimate perfection in the metamorphosing process from chaos to precious stone, symbol of purposeful evolution, evoking the Jeweled City of the New Jerusalem. The "translucent....flowers, not one of which fades" refer to realms beyond the physical and material. It was the Poet's task to illumine those realms. Thus Gautier becomes a symbol for Mallarmé's ideal.

The above will give the reader a small idea of the depths and facets which are inherent in the small space of a Mallarméan poem.

In his work may be experienced a refinement of language, a loftiness of metaphor, a genius for invention. His recurring symbols are like metamorphosing melodies in a symphony, uniting the individual poems into a unified whole wherein appear familiar guiding signposts. Some of his poems may actually be experienced as a transubstantiation to the luminosity of what he called "the glory" which he understood so well. These become meditations in which the poet participates as they unfold before the reader who does the same.

Such comprehension is admittedly difficult and requires an intelligent, passionate reader. There is reason why several poems in the present volume have never before or have rarely been translated, and why André Gide called "Un Coup De Dés" (A Throw of the Dice) "the most untranslatable poem in any language." Previous translators perhaps were not familiar with the works of renowned philosophers which Mallarmé was able to study in translation. Such a one was Georg Hegel, who dealt with an advanced spiritual concept concerning the process of human cognition, unfamiliar to the materialist thinkers of the period. Mallarmé's work reveals a profound concern with those concepts, transformed into imaginations. Thus he became a seismograph for the dawning of new spiritual awakening at the close of the nineteenth century, which some have called "Michaelic." This does not imply that the reader is required to study Hegel in order to appreciate the poetry of Mallarmé. Great works of art exist on many levels and remain forever "avant garde." Time does not exhaust, but instead enhances their significance. Wider knowledge (in which *œuvres* themselves are instruments of bringing about) leads one to ever new levels of comprehension.

"Un Coup De Dés" opened possibilities for future poets for embodying more lofty concepts. "A Tomb for Anatole" is so "avant garde" that even in our time few have deciphered its expression in poetry and structure the way one might deal with realms beyond death. It is no wonder that such intensity caused the poet the "agonizing birth pangs" he suffered in his nightly vigils by his "lamp."

Mallarmé himself became the Hamlet (one of his major symbols) who, in his "plumed toque" (Plume as upright feather—vertical self—and as Pen—the word), stands in isolation on his "roc" (reef), wailing into the Abyss ("L'Abîme") which is about to sweep him into oblivion with all Earth being, and which he, against his will, has been destined to overcome. Within is locked the "virgin symbol" about to be born (Light out of Darkness) and can be born only if he makes that "throw of the dice" which will bring harmony out of the chaos of the whirlwind which is sweeping humanity into the whirlpool. For Mallarmé, the dice throw was the creative work of Art—Poetry. He understood that Poetry could lead to the salvation of humankind for through it we may ascend into the imaginative realm beyond the material, a step necessary for the evolution of consciousness. In agony, he made that dice-throw, thereby naming the divinity which he struggled so to realize. He himself became that rare genius, born of a "constellation" wherein genius has its source. Out of profound suffering, he forged jewels which ascend into that "Silence" beyond the clamor of the "Here-below," that "Absent" realm which he succeeded in defining. Thus his poems are resolutions which end the discord between flesh and spirit, so exquisitely expressed in "Canticle of Saint John."

Although rejected by the mature and popular poets of his time, Mallarmé gathered about himself a group of younger poets who were to carry forth his vision. On June 1, 1872, he announced his literary afternoons for young persons. Among those present were Henri de Régnier, Albert Mockel, Pierre Louys, Paul Claudel, Edmund Dujardin, Emile Verhaeren, Francis Vielé-Griffin, and Paul Valéry. They had the good fortune to experience his wit, his elegance, his originality, his grace, and his insight.

Mallarmé considered the Poet as a magician, a guardian of the mysteries as were the Initiates of old. His symbols are those of prophecy, of dream, of the void, constellations, mirrors—a world beyond the "Ici-bas" (the Here-below). He understood Shadow, transmutation, multiplicity, ambiguity of meaning, and he strove for purity. He succeeded in creating a world beyond the merely temporal and physical. Though scorned and rejected, he never lost confidence in a future which would be capable of penetrating to his own ideal. His confidence was justified. Today Mallarmé is considered to be one of the greatest poetic geniuses of world literature.

His poem "Salut," composed near the close of his life, which he recited at a dinner for *La Plume*, a literary periodical, eloquently expresses his legacy to the young:

....We are sailing, O my various
Friends, I already on the stern
You, the sumptuous prow which cuts
The tide of thunderbolts and winters;

A lovely intoxication urges me
Fearless of the pitching
To offer upright this toast.

Solitude, reef, star
To whatever was worthy
Of the white concern of our sail.

The influence of Stéphane Mallarmé's poetry on all subsequent poetry has yet to be measured.

—*Daisy Aldan*

Table of Contents

To Purify the Words of the Tribe

Apparition

LA lune s'attristait. Des séraphins en pleurs
Rêvant, l'archet aux doigts, dans le calme des fleurs
Vaporeuses, tiraient de mourantes violes
De blancs sanglots glissant sur l'azur des corolles.
—C'était le jour béni de ton premier baiser.
Ma songerie aimant à me martyriser
S'enivrait savamment du parfum de tristesse
Que même sans regret et sans déboire laisse
La cueillaison d'un Rêve au cœur qui l'a cueilli.
J'errais donc, l'œil rivé sur le pavé vieilli
Quand avec du soleil aux cheveux, dans la rue
Et dans le soir, tu m'es en riant apparue
Et j'ai cru voir la fée au chapeau de clarté
Qui jadis sur mes beaux sommeils d'enfant gâté
Passait, laissant toujours de ses mains mal fermées
Neiger de blancs bouquets d'étoiles parfumées.

Apparition

THE moon grew sorrowful. Weeping Seraphim
Dreaming with drawn bows, in the calm of misty
Flowers, drew from expiring viols
White sobs gliding across azure corollas.
—It was the blessed day of your first kiss.
My musing delighting to torment me
Was drinking deep of the perfume of sadness
Which even without regret or deception, leaves to the heart
Which has gathered it, the reaping of a dream.
I wandered then, eyes glued to the worn pavement
When with sunlight in your hair, in the street
And in the evening, laughing, you appeared
And I thought I saw the fairy in her cap of light
Who once in my tranquil spoiled-child sleep
Passed by, and who from her half-closed hands
Let snow down white bouquets of perfumed stars.

Le Guignon

AU-DESSUS du bétail ahuri des humains
Bondissaient en clartés les sauvages crinières
Des mendieurs d'azur le pied dans nos chemins.

Un noir vent sur leur marche éployé pour bannières
La flagellait de froid tel jusque dans la chair,
Qu'il y creusait aussi d'irritables ornières.

Toujours avec l'espoir de rencontrer la mer,
Ils voyageaient sans pain, sans bâtons et sans urnes,
Mordant au citron d'or de l'idéal amer.

La plupart râla dans les défilés nocturnes,
S'enivrant du bonheur de voir couler son sang,
O Mort le seul baiser aux bouches tactiturnes!

Leur défaite, c'est par un ange très puissant
Debout à l'horizon dans le nu de son glaive:
Une pourpre se caille au sein reconnaissant.

Ils tettent la douleur comme ils tétaient le rêve
Et quand ils vont rythmant des pleurs voluptueux
Le peuple s'agenouille et leur mère se lève.

Ceux-là sont consolés, sûrs et majestueux;
Mais traînent à leurs pas cent frères qu'on bafoue,
Dérisoires martyrs de hasards tortueux.

Le sel pareil des pleurs ronge leur douce joue,
Ils mangent de la cendre avec le même amour,
Mais vulgaire ou bouffon le destin qui les roue.

Ils pouvaient exciter aussi comme un tambour
La servile pitié des races à voix ternes,
Egaux de Prométhée à qui manque un vautour!

The Jinx

ABOVE the bewildered herd of humans
The wild manes of the supplicants for the Azure
Feet on our paths, leapt in light.

A foul wind, their banner, unfurled for their march,
Whipped them with such a piercing cold
That it chiseled raw grooves into the flesh.

With dauntless hope of reaching the sea,
They journeyed without bread, without staffs or crocks,
Gnawing the golden lemon of the bitter ideal.

Most suffered death-throes in passage by night,
Drunk with relief to see their blood flow,
O Death, the sole kiss for voiceless mouths!

Their defeat was by a mighty Angel
With a naked sword, erect on the horizon:
A purple clots on their grateful breast.

They suck at Grief's breast as they sucked at the dream
And when they put lustful laments into verse,
The crowd bows low and their mother arises.

Such are consoled, secure and majestic;
But drag at their heels a hundred scorned brothers,
Pitiful martyrs of tortuous hazards.

The same salt-tears gnaw their gentle cheek,
They consume ashes with the self-same love,
But vulgarian or buffoon is the fate which flogs them.

Like a beating drum they too might arouse
The servile pity of wan-voiced tribes,
Equals of Prometheus who lack a vulture!

Non, vils et fréquentant les déserts sans citerne,
Ils courent sous le fouet d'un monarque rageur,
Le Guignon, dont le rire inouï les prosterne.

Amants, il saute en croupe à trois, le partageur!
Puis le torrent franchi, vous plonge en une mare
Et laisse un bloc boueux du blanc couple nageur.

Grâce à lui, si l'un souffle à son buccin bizarre,
Des enfants nous tordront en un rire obstiné
Qui, le poing à leur cul, singeront sa fanfare.

Grâce à lui, si l'urne orne à point un sein fané
Par une rose qui nubile le rallume,
De la bave luira sur son bouquet damné.

Et ce squelette nain, coiffé d'un feutre à plume
Et botté, dont l'aisselle a pour poils vrais des vers,
Est pour eux l'infini de la vaste amertume.

Vexés ne vont-ils pas provoquer le pervers,
Leur rapière grinçant suit le rayon de lune
Qui neige en sa carcasse et qui passe au travers.

Désolés sans l'orgueil qui sacre l'infortune,
Et tristes de venger leurs os de coups de bec,
Ils convoitent la haine, au lieu de la rancune.

Ils sont l'amusement des racleurs de rebec,
Des marmots, de putains et de la vieille engeance
Des loqueteux dansant quand le broc est à sec.

Les poètes bons pour l'aumône ou la vengeance,
Ne connaissant le mal de ces dieux effacés,
Les disent ennuyeux et sans intelligence.

«Ils peuvent fuir ayant de chaque exploit assez,
»Comme un vierge cheval écume de tempête
»Plutôt que de partir en galops cuirassés.

No, abject and haunting waterless deserts,
They run beneath the lash of a raging tyrant,
The Jinx whose weird laughter bows them low.

He leaps behind two lovers, a third, to split them!
The torrent crossed, plunges you in a pond
And leaves in a muddy lump the white pair of swimmers.

Thanks to him, if one blows one's bizarre trumpet,
The children will convulse us with persistent laughter,
Fists stuck in their rear will ape his flourish.

If the urn rightly adorns a shrunken breast,
Which a ripened rose rekindles,
Some slime will gleam on the cursed bouquet.

And this dwarf skeleton, crowned with a plumed toque
And booted, in whose armpits are worms instead of hairs,
Is for them the infinite of endless bitterness.

Angered, will they not challenge the pervert,
Their grating rapier follows the moonray
Which snows on his carcass and passes through it.

Desolate without pride which hallows adversity
And sad to avenge their bones with jibes,
They covet hatred instead of rancor.

They are the dupes of scrapers of fiddles,
Of urchins, of whores and of the old brood
Of swagmen who dance when the jug runs dry.

Those poets adept at alms and revenge,
Know not the pain of these vanished gods,
And call them dull and say they are stupid.

"They can flee fed-up with each exploit,
Like a virgin horse who fumes up a storm
Rather than set off in an iron-clad gallop.

»Nous soûlerons d'encens le vainqueur dans la fête:
»Mais eux, pourquoi n'endosser pas, ces baladins,
»D'écarlate haillon hurant que l'on s'arrête!»

Quand en face tous leur ont craché les dédains,
Nuls et la barbe à mots bas priant le tonnerre,
Ces héros excédés de malaises badins

Vont ridiculement se pendre au réverbère.

We'll sate with incense the victor in the feast;
As for them, why not harness these clowns
With scarlet tatters until they howl, —Stop!"

When all have spit their contempt in their faces,
Ciphers, their beards muttering a prayer to the thunder,
These heroes fed up with gibing stresses,

Ridiculously, go hang themselves on the lampposts.

Placet Futile

PRINCESSE! à jalouser le destin d'une Hébé
Qui poind sur cette tasse au baiser de vos lèvres,
J'use mes feux mais n'ai rang discret que d'abbé
Et ne figurerai même nu sur le Sèvres.

Comme je ne suis pas ton bichon embarbé,
Ni la pastille ni du rouge, ni jeux mièvres
Et que sur moi je sais ton regard clos tombé,
Blonde dont les coiffeurs divins sont des orfèvres!

Nommez-nous.... toi de qui tant de ris framboisés
Se joignent en troupeau d'agneaux apprivoisés
Chez tous broutant les vœux et bêlant aux délires,

Nommez-nous.... pour qu'Amour ailé d'un éventail
M'y peigne flûte aux doigts endormant ce bercail,
Princesse, nommez-nous berger de vos sourires.

Futile Petition

PRINCESS! jealous of the fate of a Hebe
Who rises on the cup to meet the kiss of your lips,
I spend my ardors but have only the modest rank of an Abbe
And will not even appear nude on the Sevres cup.

As I am not your bewhiskered lapdog,
Nor pastille nor lipstick, nor parlor games
And am aware of your closed glance falling on me,
Blonde whose divine coiffeurs are goldsmiths!

Appoint us.... you whose many raspberry smiles
Are joined by a flock of tamed lambs
All nibbling the vows and bleating at ecstasies,

Appoint us.... so that Love winged with a fan
Portrays me there, flute in my fingers, lulling this fold,
Princess, appoint us shepherd of your smiles.

Le Pitre Chatié

YEUX, lacs avec ma simple ivresse de renaître
Autre que l'histrion qui du geste évoquais
Comme plume la suie ignoble des quinquets,
J'ai troué dans le mur de toile une fenêtre.

De ma jambe et des bras limpide nageur traître,
A bonds multilpliés, reniant le mauvais
Hamlet! c'est comme si dans l'onde j'innovais
Mille sépulcres pour y vierge disparaître.

Hilare or de cymbale à des poings irrité,
Tout à coup le soleil frappe la nudité
Qui pure s'exhala de ma fraîcheur de nacre,

Rance nuit de la peau quand sur moi vous passiez,
Ne sachant pas, ingrat! que c'était tout mon sacre,
Ce fard noyé dans l'eau perfide des glaciers.

The Clown Reproved

EYES, lakes with my simple rapture to be reborn
Other than the performer who with a gesture
Evoked as quill the vile soot of the spotlights,
I have pierced a window in the canvas wall.

With my leg and my arms, limpid deceitful swimmer,
With multiple leaps, denying the poor
Hamlet! as if in the water I created
A thousand sepulchres to vanish there as virgin.

Jubilant gold of the cymbal struck by fists,
All at once the sun strikes the nakedness
Which exhaled pure from my nacreous freshness.

Rancid night of the skin, when you passed over me,
Unaware, ingrate! that this greasepaint drowned
In treacherous water of glaciers was my sole crown.

Une négresse par le démon secouée....

UNE négresse par le démon secouée
Veut goûter une enfant triste de fruits nouveaux
Et criminels aussi sous leur robe trouée,
Cette goinfre s'apprête à de rusés travaux:

A son ventre compare heureuses deux tétines
Et, si haut que la main ne le saura saisir,
Elle darde le choc obscur de ses bottines
Ainsi que quelque langue inhabile au plaisir.

Contre la nudité peureuse de gazelle
Qui tremble, sur le dos tel un fol éléphant
Renversée elle attend et s'admire avec zèle,
En riant de ses dents naïves à l'enfant;

Et, dans ses jambes où la victime se couche,
Levant une peau noire ouverte sous le crin,
Avance le palais de cette étrange bouche
Pâle et rose comme un coquillage marin.

A Negress possessed by a demon....

A Negress possessed by a demon
Desires to taste a child weary of strange
And evil fruits beneath their tattered robe;
This glutton prepares with cunning tricks:

At her belly she compares two jolly teats
And, so high that the hand cannot seize it,
She darts forth the dark shock between her booted legs
Like some tongue unskilled in pleasure.

Near the timid nudity of a gazelle
Trembling like a wild elephant, flat on her back,
She pauses, and admires herself with gusto,
Laughing with her white teeth at the child;

And, between her legs where the victim lies,
Raising a black skin open beneath the tuft,
She thrusts the palate of that singular mouth
Pale and pink as a seashell.

Les Fenêtres

LAS du triste hôpital, et de l'encens fétide
Qui monte en la blancheur banale des rideaux
Vers le grand crucifix ennuyé du mur vide,
Le moribond sournois y redresse un vieux dos,

Se traîne et va, moins pour chauffer sa pourriture
Que pour voir du soleil sur les pierres, coller
Les poils blancs et les os de la maigre figure
Aux fenêtres qu'un beau rayon clair veut hâler.

Et la bouche, fiévreuse et d'azur bleu vorace,
Telle, jeune, elle alla respirer son trésor,
Une peau virginale et de jadis! encrasse
D'un long baiser amer les tièdes carreaux d'or.

Ivre, il vit, oubliant l'horreur des saintes huiles,
Les tisanes, l'horoge et le lit infligé,
La toux; et quand le soir saigne parmi les tuiles,
Son œil, à l'horizon de lumière gorgé,

Voit des galères d'or, belles comme des cygnes,
Sur un fleuve de pourpre et de parfums dormir
En berçant l'éclair fauve et riche de leurs lignes
Dans un grand nonchaloir chargé de souvenir!

Ainsi, pris du dégoût de l'homme à l'âme dure
Vautré dans le bonheur, où ses seuls appétits
Mangent, et qui s'entête à chercher cette ordure
Pour l'offrir à la femme allaitant ses petits,

Je fuis et je m'accroche à toutes les croisées
D'où l'on tourne l'épaule à la vie, et, béni,
Dans leur verre, lavé d'éternelles rosées,
Que dore le matin chaste de l'Infini

Windows

SICK of the dreary hospital, and the rank fumes
Rising with the banal whiteness of the curtains
Toward the great crucifix; weary of the bare wall,
The sullen dying man straightens his old spine,

Shuffles, less to warm his rotting body
Than to see the sun on the stones, to press
His white hairs and the bones of his skeletal face
To the panes which a lovely clear ray wants to tinge,

And his mouth, feverish and greedy for the azure,
As when young, it leaned to inhale its beloved,
A virginal cheek of yore, soils
With a long bitter kiss the warm golden panes.

Drunk, forgetting the horror of the holy oils,
The herb teas, the clock and the imposed bed,
The cough, he lives again; and when twilight bleeds on the tiles,
His eye, on the horizon gorged with light,

Sees golden galleys, beautiful as swans,
Sleeping on a perfumed river of crimson
Rocking the rich fauve flash of their lines
In a great calm charged with memory!

Thus, disgusted with the blunt-souled man
Who wallows in comforts, where his appetites alone
Are fed, and who insists on fetching this filth
To present to his wife nursing her children,

I flee and I cling to all those windows
From where one turns in scorn from life, and hallowed,
In their glass, washed by eternal dews,
Gilded by the chaste morning of the Infinite

Je me mire et me vois ange! et je meurs, et j'aime
—Que la vitre soit l'art, soit la mysticité—
A renaître, portant mon rêve en diadème,
Au ciel antérieur où fleurit la Beauté!

Mais, hélas! Ici-bas est maître: sa hantise
Vient m'écœurer parfois jusqu'en cet abri sûr,
Et le vomissement impur de la Bêtise
Me force à me boucher le nez devant l'azur.

Est-il moyen, ô Moi qui connais l'amertume,
D'enfoncer le cristal par le monstre insulté
Et de m'enfuir, avec mes deux ailes sans plume
—Au risque de tomber pendant l'éternité?

I see myself as Angel, and I die, and I long
—Let the glass be art, let it be mysticism—
To be reborn, wearing my dream as a crown,
In an earlier heaven where Beauty flourished!

But, alas! Here-below is master: its obsession
Nauseates me even in this safe retreat,
And the foul vomit of Stupidity
Compels me to hold my nose before the azure.

Is there a way, O Self who knows bitterness,
Which the monster offends, to shatter the crystal
And to escape with my two featherless wings
—At the risk of falling away in eternity?

Les Fleurs

DES avalanches d'or du vieil azur, au jour
Premier et de la neige éternelle des astres
Jadis tu détachas les grands calices pour
La terre jeune encore et vierge de désastres,

Le glaïeul fauve, avec les cygnes au col fin,
Et ce divin laurier des âmes exilées
Vermeil comme le pur orteil du séraphin
Que rougit la pudeur des aurores foulées,

L'hyacinthe, le myrte à l'adorable éclair
Et, pareille à la chair de la femme, la rose
Cruelle, Hérodiade en fleur du jardin clair,
Celle qu'un sang farouche et radieux arrose!

Et tu fis la blancheur sanglotante des lys
Qui roulant sur des mers de soupirs qu'elle effleure
A travers l'encens bleu des horizons pâlis
Monte rêveusement vers la lune qui pleure!

Hosannah sur le cistre et dans les encensoirs,
Notre Dame, hosannah du jardin de nos limbes!
Et finisse l'écho par les célestes soirs,
Extase des regards, scintillement des nimbes!

O Mère qui créas en ton sein juste et fort,
Calices balançant la future fiole,
De grandes fleurs avec la balsamique Mort
Pour le poète las que la vie étiole.

The Flowers

FROM the golden avalanches of the ancient azure,
On the primal day, and from the eternal snow of the stars
Once you released the great calyxes for
The still youthful earth, virgin of disasters,

The fauve gladiolus, with the slender throated swans,
And the divine laurel of exiled souls
Vermilion like the pristine toe of a Seraph
Which the modesty of trampled dawns crimsons,

The hyacinth, the myrtle with its heavenly flash
And, like the flesh of woman, the cruel
Rose, flowering Herodias of the limpid garden,
She who is bedewed with savage and lustrous blood!

And you fashioned the sobbing white of the lily
Which rolling over the seas of sighs that it brushes,
Across blue incense of pale horizons
Dreamily ascends toward the weeping moon!

Hosannah on the cithern and in the censers,
Our Lady, Hosannah from the garden of our limbos!
And may the echo cease during the celestial evenings
Ecstasy of glances, nimbus scintillations!

O Mother who created in your mighty and righteous bosom,
Calyxes balancing the future phial,
Majestic flowers with balsamic Death
For the weary poet, wasted by life.

Renouveau

L E printemps maladif a chassé tristement
L'hiver, saison de l'art serein, l'hiver lucide,
Et, dans mon être à qui le sang morne préside
L'impuissance s'étire en un long bâillement.

Des crépuscules blancs tiédissent sous mon crâne
Qu'un cercle de fer serre ainsi qu'un vieux tombeau
Et triste, j'erre après un rêve vague et beau,
Par les champs où la sève immense se pavane

Puis je tombe énervé de parfums d'arbres, las,
Et creusant de ma face une fosse à mon rêve,
Mordant la terre chaude où poussent les lilas,

J'attends, en m'abîmant que mon ennui s'élève....
—Cependant l'Azur rit sur la haie et l'éveil
De tant d'oiseaux en fleur gazouillant au soleil.

Renewal

SADLY, the sickly Spring has banished
Winter, season of placid art, the lucid Winter,
And in my being, where my dismal blood presides
Impotence stretches in a slow yawn.

White twilights grow tepid within my skull
Which an iron ring grips like an ancient tomb
And sorrowfully, I wander after a vague, lofty dream,
Through the fields where a splendid dew is preening.

Then I sink down, faint from the perfume of trees, spent,
And hollowing with my face a grave for my dream,
Gnawing the warm earth where the lilacs grow,

Then engulfed, I wait for my ennui to lift....
—Yet the Azure laughs upon the hedge and the waking
Of so many birds in flower chirping in the sunlight.

Angoisse

JE ne viens pas ce soir vaincre ton corps, ô bête
En qui vont les péchés d'un peuple, ni creuser
Dans tes cheveux impurs une triste tempête
Sous l'incurable ennui que verse mon baiser:

Je demande à ton lit le lourd sommeil sans songes
Planant sous les rideaux inconnus du remords,
Et que tu peux goûter après tes noirs mensonges,
Toi qui sur le néant en sais plus que les morts.

Car le Vice, rongeant ma native noblesse
M'a comme toi marqué de sa stérilité,
Mais tandis que ton sein de pierre est habité

Par un cœur que la dent d'aucun crime ne blesse,
Je fuis, pâle, défait, hanté par mon linceul,
Ayant peur de mourir lorsque je couche seul.

Anguish

I come tonight not to conquer your body, O creature
In whom course a people's sins, nor to burrow
In your tainted hair a dismal tempest
Beneath the fatal ennui poured by my kiss.

I ask of your bed the heavy sleep without dreams
Of remorse hovering beneath the unfamiliar curtains,
And which you too may savor after your dark lies,
You who know more of the void than the dead.

For Vice, gnawing at my innate nobility
Has branded me as you with its sterility,
But while in your breast of stone there lives

A heart that the tooth of no crime can despoil,
I flee, pale, broken, haunted by my shroud,
In fear of dying when I sleep alone.

Las de l'amer repos....

L AS de l'amer repos où ma paresse offense
Une gloire pour qui jadis j'ai fui l'enfance
Adorable des bois de roses sous l'azur
Naturel, et plus las sept fois du pacte dur
De creuser par veillée une fosse nouvelle
Dans le terrain avare et froid de ma cervelle,
Fossoyeur sans pitié pour la stérilité,
—Que dire à cette Aurore, ô Rêves, visité
Par les roses, quand, peur de ses roses livides,
Le vaste cimetière unira les trous vides?—

Je veux délaisser l'Art vorace d'un pays
Cruel, et, souriant aux reproches vieillis
Que me font mes amis, le passé, le génie,
Et ma lampe qui sait pourtant mon agonie,
Imiter le Chinois au cœur limpide et fin
De qui l'extase pure est de peindre la fin
Sur ses tasses de neige à la lune ravie
D'une bizarre fleur qui parfume sa vie
Transparente, la fleur qu'il a sentie, enfant,
Au filigrane bleu de l'âme se greffant.
Et, la mort telle avec le seul rêve du sage,
Serein, je vais choisir un jeune paysage
Que je peindrais encor sur les tasses, distrait.
Une ligne d'azur mince et pâle serait
Un lac, parmi le ciel de porcelaine nue,
Un clair croissant perdu par une blanche nue
Trempe sa corne calme en la glace des eaux,
Non loin de trois grands cils d'émeraude, roseaux.

Weary of the bitter repose....

WEARY of the bitter repose where my indolence offends
A glory for which once I fled adorable
Childhood of rose-filled groves beneath the azure
Of Nature, and more than seven times weary of the onerous pact
Of digging, sleepless nights, a new groove
In the miserly and frozen terrain of my brain,
Sexton without pity for sterility,
—Visited by roses, what shall I say to this Dawn,
O Dreams, when, fearful of its own livid roses,
The vast cemetery will unite the empty graves?—

I would leave voracious Art of a cruel
Country, and scorning the outworn reproaches
Of my friends, the past, genius,
And my lamp which knows of my anguish,
Imitate the Chinese of limpid and delicate heart
Whose unsullied ecstasy lies in painting
On his cup, white as moon-ravished snow
The death of a bizarre flower which perfumes his life
Transparent, the flower he felt as a child
Incised on the blue filigrane of his soul.
And with a death like the sole dream of the Sage,
Serenely, I'll choose a youthful landscape
Which I'd paint again on the cups, with an absent air.
A line of blue, thin and pale would be
A lake, amid the sky of virgin porcelain,
A clear crescent moon lost in a white cloud
Dips its tranquil horn in the ice of the waters,
Not far from three great emerald eyelashes, reeds.

Le Sonneur

CEPENDANT que la cloche éveille sa voix claire
A l'air pur et limpide et profond du matin
Et passe sur l'enfant qui jette pour lui plaire
Un angélus parmi la lavande et le thym,

Le sonneur effleuré par l'oiseau qu'il éclaire,
Chevauchant tristement en geignant du latin
Sur la pierre qui tend la corde séculaire,
N'entend descendre à lui qu'un tintement lointain.

Je suis cet homme. Hélas! de la nuit désireuse,
J'ai beau tirer le câble à sonner l'Idéal,
De froids péchés s'ébat un plumage féal,

Et la voix ne me vient que par bribes et creuse!
Mais, un jour, fatigué d'avoir en vain tiré,
O Satan, j'ôterai la pierre et me pendrai.

The Bell Ringer

WHILE the bell quickens its clear voice
In the pure, limpid and sharp morning air
And glides over the child who to oblige it, scatters
An angelus among the lavender and thyme,

The bell ringer grazed by the bird he illumines,
Stumbling wretchedly and grumbling Latin
Against the stone which tenses the ancient cord,
Hears only a distant tinkling reaching his ears.

I am that man, alas! Of anxious night,
In vain I tug the cable to ring out the Ideal,
A trusty plumage of cold sins rollicks about,

And my voice rises only in snatches and hollow!
But, one day, exhausted from having tugged in vain,
O Satan, I will unhitch the stone and hang myself.

Tristesse d'Été

LE soleil, sur le sable, ô lutteuse endormie,
En l'or de tes cheveux chauffe un bain langoureux
Et, consumant l'encens sur ta joue ennemie,
Il mêle avec les pleurs un breuvage amoureux.

De ce blanc flamboiement l'immuable accalmie
T'a fait dire, attristée, ô mes baisers peureux,
«Nous ne serons jamais une seule momie
Sous l'antique désert et les palmiers heureux!»

Mais ta chevelure est une rivière tiède,
Où noyer sans frissons l'âme qui nous obsède
Et trouver ce Néant que tu ne connais pas!

Je goûterai le fard pleuré par tes paupières,
Pour voir s'il sait donner au cœur que tu frappas
L'insensibilité de l'azur et des pierres.

Summer Sadness

O sleeping wrestler, on the sand, the sunlight
Heats a languorous bath in the gold of your hair
And, inhaling the incense on your hostile cheek,
It mingles an amorous potion with your tears.

The immutable calm of this white blaze
(O my timid kisses) made you sadly declare,
"We will never be a single mummy
Beneath the ancient desert and the happy palms!"

But your tresses are a tepid river
Wherein our soul obsessed may drown without trembling
And find the Void which you do not fathom!

I will taste the kohl wept by your tears,
To see if it can bestow on this heart you have wounded
The indifference of the azure, and stones.

L'*Azur*

De l'éternel azur la sereine ironie
Accable, belle indolemment comme les fleurs,
Le poète impuissant qui maudit son génie
A travers un désert stérile de Douleurs.

Fuyant, les yeux fermés, je le sens qui regarde
Avec l'intensité d'un remords atterrant,
Mon âme vide. Où fuir? Et quelle nuit hagarde
Jeter, lambeaux, jeter sur ce mépris navrant?

Brouillards, montez! Versez vos cendres monotones
Avec de longs haillons de brume dans les cieux
Qui noiera le marais livide des automnes
Et bâtissez un grand plafond silencieux!

Et toi, sors des étangs léthéens et ramasse
En t'en venant la vase et les pâles roseaux,
Cher Ennui, pour boucher d'une main jamais lasse
Les grands trous bleus que font méchamment les oiseaux.

Encor! que sans répit les tristes cheminées
Fument, et que de suie une errante prison
Eteigne dans l'horreur de ses noires traînées
Le soleil se mourant jaunâtre à l'horizon!

—Le Ciel est mort.—Vers toi, j'accours! donne, ô matière,
L'oubli de l'Idéal cruel et du Péché
A ce martyr qui vient partager la litière
Où le bétail heureux des hommes est couché,

Car j'y veux, puisque enfin ma cervelle, vidée
Comme le pot de fard gisant au pied d'un mur,
N'a plus l'art d'attifer la sanglotante idée,
Lugubrement bâiller vers un trépas obscur....

The Azure

THE serene irony of the infinite azure
Languorously lovely as flowers, crushes
The impotent poet who curses his genius
Across a sterile desert of Sorrows.

Fleeing, eyes shut, I feel it glaring
Fierce as a shattering remorse
At my empty soul. Where flee? And what haggard night
Cast, torn shrouds, cast over this heart-rending scorn?

Fogs, rise! Pour your monotonous ashes
With long tatters of mist across the sky
To drown the livid swamp of autumns
And fashion a vast silent ceiling!

And you, emerge from the Lethean ponds and gather
On your way, the mire and the pale reeds,
Dear Ennui, to stop up with a tireless hand
The vast blue breaches maliciously rent by the birds.

Still more! Let the dreary smokestacks ceaselessly
Pour smoke, and let a roving prison of soot
Blot out in the horror of its dismal trains
The sun dying in sulfur on the horizon!

—The Sky is dead.—Toward you, I hasten! Bestow, O matter,
Oblivion of the cruel Ideal and of Sin
Upon this martyr who comes to share the litter
Where the contented herd of humans lies asleep,

For there I desire, since at last my brain, emptied
Like the pot of greasepaint left lying at the base of a wall,
Has lost the art to adorn the sobbing idea,
To yawn in mourning toward an obscure death....

En vain! l'Azur triomphe, et je l'entends qui chante
Dans les cloches. Mon âme, il se fait voix pour plus
Nous faire peur avec sa victoire méchante,
Et du métal vivant sort en bleus angélus!

Il roule par la brume, ancien et traverse
Ta native agonie ainsi qu'un glaive sûr;
Où fuir dans la révolte inutile et perverse?
Je suis hanté. L'Azur! L'Azur! L'Azur! L'Azur!

In vain! The Azure triumphs, and I hear it singing
In the bells. It assumes a voice to frighten
Us anew, my Soul, with its wicked victory
And from the vibrant metal soars in blue angeluses!

Ancient, it rolls in the fog, and cleaves
Your innate agony like an unerring sword;
Where flee in this futile and perverse revolt?
I am haunted! The Azure! The Azure! The Azure! The Azure!

Brise Marine

LA chair est triste, hélas! et j'ai lu tous les livres.
Fuir! là-bas fuir! Je sens que des oiseaux sont ivres
D'être parmi l'écume inconnue et les cieux!
Rien, ni les vieux jardins reflétés par les yeux
Ne retiendra ce cœur qui dans la mer se trempe
O nuits! ni la clarté déserte de ma lampe
Sur le vide papier que la blancheur défend
Et ni la jeune femme allaitant son enfant.
Je partirai! Steamer balançant ta mâture,
Lève l'ancre pour une exotique nature!

Un Ennui, désolé par les cruels espoirs,
Croit encore à l'adieu suprême des mouchoirs!
Et, peut-être, les mâts, invitant les orages
Sont-ils de ceux qu'un vent penche sur les naufrages
Perdus, sans mâts, sans mâts, ni fertiles îlots....
Mais, ô mon cœur, entends le chant des matelots!

Sea Breeze

THE flesh is sad, alas! and I've read all the books.
To escape! To flee far away! I sense the birds drunk
With joy to be amid foreign foam and skies!
Naught, neither ancient gardens the eyes reflect
Can contain this heart, steeped in the sea
O nights! nor the solitary light of my lamp
On the blank sheet which its whiteness shields
Nor the young wife nursing her child.
I shall depart! Steamer with your swaying masts,
Lift anchor for an exotic landscape!

An Ennui, ravaged by cruel expectations,
Still believes in the final *adieux* of handkerchiefs!
And, perhaps, the masts inviting the tempests
Are such as a gale bends toward shipwrecks
Lost, without masts, no masts, no fertile isles....
But, O my heart, listen to the sailor's song!

Soupir

Mon âme vers ton front où rêve, ô calme sœur,
Un automne jonché de taches de rousseur,
Et vers le ciel errant de ton œil angélique
Monte, comme dans un jardin mélancolique,
Fidèle, un blanc jet d'eau soupire vers l'Azur!
—Vers l'Azur attendri d'Octobre pâle et pur
Qui mire aux grands bassins sa langueur infinie
Et laisse, sur l'eau morte où la fauve agonie
Des feuilles erre au vent et creuse un froid sillon,
Se traîner le soleil jaune d'un long rayon.

Sigh

TOWARD your brow where dreams, O calm sister,
An autumn strewn with russet freckles
And toward the errant sky of your angelic eye
My soul ascends, as in a melancholy garden,
Faithful, a white jet of water sighs toward the Azure!
—Toward the Azure softened by a pale and pure October
Which mirrors in the great pools its infinite languor,
And, on the dead water where the fauve agony
Of leaves wanders in the wind, and carves a cold furrow,
Lets trail in a long lingering ray the yellow sun.

Aumône

Prends ce sac, Mendiant! tu ne le cajolas
Sénile nourrisson d'une tétine avare
Afin de pièce à pièce en égoutter ton glas.

Tire du métal cher quelque péché bizarre
Et vaste comme nous, les poings pleins, le baisons
Souffles-y qu'il se torde! une ardente fanfare.

Eglise avec l'encens que toutes ces maisons
Sur les murs quand berceur d'une bleue éclaircie
Le tabac sans parler roule les oraisons,

Et l'opium puissant brise la pharmacie!
Robes et peau, veux-tu lacérer le satin
Et boire en la salive heureuse l'inertie,

Par les cafés princiers attendre le matin?
Les plafonds enrichis de nymphes et de voiles,
On jette, au mendiant de la vitre, un festin.

Et quand tu sors, vieux dieu, grelottant sous tes toiles
D'emballage, l'aurore est un lac de vin d'or
Et tu jures avoir au gosier les étoiles!

Faute de supputer l'éclat de ton trésor,
Tu peux du moins t'orner d'une plume, à complies
Servir un cierge au saint en qui tu crois encor.

Ne t'imagine pas que je dis des folies.
La terre s'ouvre vieille à qui crève la faim.
Je hais une autre aumône et veux que tu m'oublies.

Et surtout ne va pas, frère, acheter du pain.

Alms

TAKE this purse, Beggar! You did not wheedle it
Senile nursling, from a stingy teat
To drain from it bit by bit your death-knell.

Extract from the costly metal some sin, bizarre
And vast, as we, our fists full, kiss it
Blow on it till it writhes! a fiery fanfare.

All these places are a church with incense
When on the walls, rocking a blue clearing
Tobacco silently rolls the oraisons.

And powerful opium eclipses the pharmacy!
Frocks and flesh! Do you desire to rip the satin
And to drink from saliva, a blissful inertia,

Awaiting the dawn in princely cafés?
Ceilings adorned with nymphs and veils,
To the beggar at the window, they toss a banquet.

And when you leave, old god, shivering in your burlap
Rags, the daybreak is a lake of golden wine
And you swear you have the stars in your gullet!

Instead of measuring the splendor of your hoard,
You can at least adorn yourself with a plume, to offer
At compline a candle to the saint in whom you still have faith.

Do not imagine that what I say is foolishness.
The earth is revealed old to a starving man.
I hate another alms and want you to forget me.

Above all, do not go, brother, to purchase bread.

Don du Poème

J E t'apporte l'enfant d'une nuit d'Idumée!
Noire, à l'aile saignante et pâle, déplumée,
Par le verre brûlé d'aromates et d'or,
Par les carreaux glacés, hélas! mornes encor,
L'aurore se jeta sur la lampe angélique.
Palmes! et quand elle a montré cette relique
A ce père essayant un sourire ennemi,
La solitude bleue et stérile a frémi.
O la berceuse, avec ta fille et l'innocence
De vos pieds froids, accueille une horrible naissance:
Et ta voix rappelant viole et clavecin,
Avec le doigt fané presseras-tu le sein
Par qui coule en blancheur sibylline la femme
Pour les lèvres que l'air du vierge azur affame?

Gift of the Poem

I bring you the child of an Idumaean night!
Black, featherless, with bleeding wing and pale,
Through the glass seared with spices and with gold,
Through the frozen panes, alas! still so bleak,
The dawn thrust itself on the angelic-lamp.
Palms! And when it had unveiled this relic
To this father essaying a hostile smile,
The blue and sterile solitude trembled.
O you, with icy feet, who cradle your daughter
And innocence, accept a ghastly birth:
And your voice evoking viol and clavacin,
Will you with your worn finger press the breast
Through which flows the sibylline whiteness of woman
For lips that are starved by the virgin azure?

Cantique de Saint Jean

Le soleil que sa halte
Surnaturelle exalte
Aussitôt redescend
    Incadescent

Je sens comme aux vertèbres
S'éployer des ténèbres
Toutes dans un frisson
    A l'unisson

Et ma tête surgie
Solitaire vigie
Dans les vols triomphaux
    De cette faux

Comme rupture franche
Plutôt refoule ou tranche
Les anciens désaccords
    Avec le corps

Qu'elle de jeûnes ivre
S'opiniâtre à suivre
En quelque bond hagard
    Son pur regard

Là-haut où la froidure
Eternelle n'endure
Que vous le surpassiez
    Tous ô glaciers

Mais selon un baptême
Illuminée au même
Principe qui m'élut
    Penche un salut.

Canticle of Saint John

THE sun exalted
By its supernal halt
Straightway redescends
          Incandescent

I feel how in my bones
Darkness begins to spread
All tremulous
          In unison

And my head as risen
Solitary vigil
In the triumphal flights
          Of this scythe

As clear rupture
Rather stems or severs
The primordial discords
          With the flesh

That drunk with fasting
Stubbornly pursues
With a haggard bound
          Its pure regard

Yonder where the eternal
Ice will not suffer
That you all surpass
          It O glaciers

But as a baptism
Illumined by the same
Word which consecrated me
          Leans down in salutation.

La chevelure....

LA chevelure vol d'une flamme à l'extrême
Occident de désirs pour la tout déployer
Se pose (je dirais mourir un diadème)
Vers le front couronné son ancien foyer

Mais sans or soupirer que cette vive nue
L'ignition du feu toujours intérieur
Originellement la seule continue
Dans le joyau de l'œil véridique ou rieur

Une nudité de héros tendre diffame
Celle qui ne mouvant astre ni feux au doigt
Rien qu'à simplifier avec gloire la femme
Accomplit par son chef fulgurante l'exploit

De semer de rubis le doute qu'elle écorche
Ainsi qu'une joyeuse et tutélaire torche.

Her mass of hair....

HER mass of hair flight of a flame to the farthest
West of desires, to have it wholly unfurl
Alights (or rather dies as diadem)
Toward the crowned brow of its former hearth

But without gold, or to sigh that this vibrant cloud
The ignition of the fire forever which remains within
(Originally the only one) continues
Within the jewel of her truthful and laughing eye

The nakedness of a tender hero defames
Her who stirring neither star nor fires on her fingers
Only to simplify the glory of womanhood
Achieves with her flashing head the daring feat

Of sowing with rubies the doubt which she sets afire
Like a joyous and guardian torch.

Sainte

A le fenêtre recélant
Le santal vieux qui se dédore
De sa viole étincelant
Jadis avec flûte ou mandore,

Est la Sainte pâle, étalant
Le livre vieux qui se déplie
Du Magnificat ruisselant
Jadis selon vêpre et complie:

A ce vitrage d'ostensoir
Que frôle une harpe par l'Ange
Formée avec son vol du soir
Pour la délicate phalange

Du doigt que, sans le vieux santal
Ni le vieux livre, elle balance
Sur le plumage instrumental,
Musicienne du silence.

Saint

AT the window ledge concealing
The old santal, gilt flaking
From her viol scintillating
Once with flute or mandore,

Stands the pale Saint, displaying
The ancient missal which unfurls
At the Magnificat, glistening
Once for vesper or compline:

At this glass pane for the monstrance
Brushed by a harp formed
By the Angel's evening flight
For the delicate fingertip

Which without the ancient santal
Nor the ancient book, she balances
On the instrumental plumage,
Musician of silence.

Toast Funèbre

O de notre bonheur, toi, le fatal emblème!

Salut de la démence et libation blême,
Ne crois pas qu'au magique espoir du corridor
J'offre ma coupe vide où souffre un monstre d'or!
Ton apparition ne va pas me suffire:
Car je t'ai mis, moi-même, en un lieu de porphyre.
Le rite est pour les mains d'éteindre le flambeau
Contre le fer épais des portes du tombeau:
Et l'on ignore mal, élu pour notre fête
Très simple de chanter l'absence du poète,
Que ce beau monument l'enferme tout entier.
Si ce n'est que la gloire ardente du métier,
Jusqu'à l'heure commune et vile de la cendre,
Par le carreau qu'allume un soir fier d'y descendre,
Retourne vers les feux du pur soleil mortel!

Magnifique, total et solitaire, tel
Tremble de s'exhaler le faux orgueil des hommes.
Cette foule hagarde! elle annonce: Nous sommes
La triste opacité de nos spectres futurs.
Mais le blason des deuils épars sur de vains murs
J'ai méprisé l'hourreur lucide d'une larme,
Quand, sourd même à mon vers sacré qui ne l'alarme
Quelqu'un de ces passants, fier, aveugle et muet,
Hôte de son linceul vague, se transmuait
En le vierge héros de l'attente posthume.
Vaste gouffre apporté dans l'amas de la brume
Par l'irascible vent des mots qu'il n'a pas dits,
Le néant à cet Homme aboli de jadis:
«Souvenirs d'horizons, qu'est-ce, ô toi, que la Terre?»
Hurle ce songe; et, voix dont la clarté s'altère,
L'espace a pour jouet le cri: «Je ne sais pas!»

Funeral Toast

OH you, fatal emblem of our felicity!

A toast of madness and a pale libation,
Think not that to the magic hope of the corridor
I offer my empty cup whereon a golden monster writhes!
Your apparition will not satisfy me:
For I, myself, have set you in a shrine of porphyry.
The rite requires the hands to quench the torch
Against the heavy iron portals of the tomb:
And we, chosen for our modest celebration
To sing the absence of the poet, can't ignore
That this monument contains him utterly.
Unless the blazing glory of his calling
Until the vile and common hour of ashes,
Through the pane inflamed by evening proudly alighting
Returns toward the fires of a pure mortal sun!

Magnificent, whole and solitary, who
Shudders to exude the false pride of men.
This haggard crowd! which proclaims: We are
The pitiful opacity of our future spectres.
But with blazons of mourning scattered on vain walls
I scorned the lucid horror of a tear,
When deaf even to my sacred verse which wakes him not,
One of those passersby, proud, blind and mute,
Inmate of his hazy shroud, might transform himself
Into the virgin hero of the posthumous hope.
Vast abyss borne into the amassing mist
By the irascible wind of his unuttered words,
Only the void for this Man made null in the past:
"Memories of horizons, O you, what is the Earth?"
Howls this dream; and in a voice whose clarity dims,
Space toys with the cry: "I know not!"

Le Maître, par un œil profond, a, sur ses pas,
Apaisé de l'éden l'inquiète merveille
Dont le frisson final, dans sa voix seule, éveille
Pour la Rose et le Lys le mystère d'un nom.
Est-il de ce destin rien qui demeure, non?
O vous tous, oubliez une croyance sombre.
Le splendide génie éternal n'a pas d'ombre.
Moi, de votre désir soucieux, je veux voir,
A qui s'évanouit, hier, dans le devoir
Idéal que nous font les jardins de cet astre,
Survivre pour l'honneur du tranquille désastre
Une agitation solennelle par l'air
De paroles, pourpre ivre et grand calice clair,
Que, pluie et diamant, le regard diaphane
Resté là sur ces fleurs dont nulle ne se fane,
Isole parmi l'heure et le rayon du jour!

C'est de nos vrais bosquets déjà tout le séjour,
Où le poète pur a pour geste humble et large
De l'interdire au rêve, ennemi de sa charge:
Afin que le matin de son repos altier,
Quand la mort ancienne et comme pour Gautier
De n'ouvrir pas les yeux sacrés et de se taire,
Surgisse, de l'allée ornement tributaire,
Le sépulcre solide où gît tout ce qui nuit,
Et l'avare silence et la massive nuit.

The Master, by his profound vision, has, in passing,
Brought calm to the troubled marvel of Eden
Where the final quiver in his voice alone, awakens
For the Rose and the Lily the mystery of a name.
Does nothing endure of this destiny, nothing?
O you all, forget so somber a belief.
Splendid eternal genius has no shade.
I, mindful of your desire, wish to see
For him who vanished yesterday, in the ideal
Duty assigned to us by the gardens of this star,
Survive in honor of the calm disaster
A solemn agitation in the air
Of words, intoxicating crimson and great clear chalice,
Which, rain and diamond, the translucent gaze
Fixed on these flowers, not one of which fades,
Isolates within the hour and the daylight glow!

Already our sole abode is in the true groves,
Where the pure poet must with grand and humble gesture
Deny it access to the dream, enemy of his task:
So that on the morning of his lofty sleep,
When antique death, as now for Gautier, means
No more to open sacred eyes and to be mute,
There may arise, tributary ornament of the alley,
The solid sepulchre where lie all that is harmful,
And niggardly-silence and the massive night.

Prose
(pour des Esseintes)

Hyperbole! de ma mémoire
Triomphalement ne sais-tu
Te lever, aujourd'hui grimoire
Dans un livre de fer vêtu:

Car j'installe, par la science,
L'hymne des cœurs spirituels
En l'œuvre de ma patience,
Atlas, herbiers et rituels.

Nous promenions notre visage
(Nous fûmes deux, je le maintiens)
Sur maints charmes de paysage,
O sœur, y comparant les tiens.

L'ère d'autorité se trouble
Lorsque, sans nul motif, on dit
De ce midi que notre double
Inconscience approfondit

Que, sol des cent iris, son site,
Ils savent s'il a bien été,
Ne porte pas de nom que cite
L'or de la trompette d'Été.

Oui, dans une île que l'air charge
De vue et non de visions
Toute fleur s'étalait plus large
Sans que nous en devisions.

Telles, immenses, que chacune
Ordinairement se para
D'un lucide contour, lacune,
Qui des jardins la sépara.

Prose
(for des Esseintes)

HYPERBOLE! Do you not know
How to rise triumphantly
From my memory, today a grimoire
In a tome bound in iron:

For I enclose, by science,
The hymn of spiritual hearts
In a labor of my patience,
Atlas, herbals and rituals.

We walked, our faces
(I maintain we were two)
Toward the landscape's many charms,
O Sister, comparing yours to them.

The Age of Authority is troubled
When, without motive, one declares
Of this noon which is fathomed
By our mutual unconscious

That, this grove of a hundred irises,
Its site, they know if it actually was,
Bears no name that is cited
By the gold of Summer's trumpet.

Yes, in an isle where the air is charged
With sight and not with fancies
Each flower unfurled with greater breadth
Without our explaining it.

All so huge, that each one
Usually was adorned
With its own luminous aura,
Hiatus which set it off from the gardens.

Gloire du long désir, Idées
Tout en moi s'exaltait de voir
La famille des iridées
Surgir à ce nouveau devoir,

Mais cette sœur sensée et tendre ,
Ne porta son regard plus loin
Que sourire et, comme à l'entendre
J'occupe mon antique soin.

Oh! sache l'Esprit de litige,
A cette heure où nous nous taisons,
Que de lis multiples la tige
Grandissait trop pour nos raisons

Et non comme pleure la rive,
Quand son jeu monotone ment
A vouloir que l'ampleur arrive
Parmi mon jeune étonnement

D'ouïr tout le ciel et la carte
Sans fin attestés sur mes pas,
Par le flot même qui s'écarte,
Que ce pays n'exista pas.

L'enfant abdique son extase
Et docte déjà par chemins
Elle dit le mot: Anastase!
Né pour d'éternels parchemins,

Avant qu'un sépulcre ne rie
Sous aucun climat, son aïeul,
De porter ce nom: Pulchérie!
Caché par le trop grand glaïeul.

Glory of long desire, Ideas
All within me rejoiced to behold
The family of the irises
Rise to this new command.

But this perceptive and tender sister
Cast her glance no further
Than to smile and, to understand her
I engage my old concern.

Oh! Let the spirit of contention know
In this hour of our silence,
That the stalk of the multiple lilies
Grew too tall for our reason.

And not as the shore weeps,
When its monotonous game plays false
In wishing for the full tide
Amid my youthful amazement

To hear the whole sky and the map
Ceaselessly attest to my steps
By the very receding wave,
That this land did not exist.

The child renounces its ecstasy
And already wise in certain ways
She speaks the word: Anastasius!
Born for eternal parchments,

Before a sepulchre beneath no clime,
Her ancestor might laugh
Bearing the name: Pulcheria!
Hidden by the overgrown gladiolus.

Éventail
(de Madame Mallarmé)

AVEC comme pour langage
Rien qu'un battement aux cieux
Le futur vers se dégage
Du logis très précieux

Aile tout bas la courrière
Cet évantail si c'est lui
Le même par qui derrière
Toi quelque miroir a lui

Limpide (où va redescendre
Pourchassée en chaque grain
Un peu d'invisible cendre
Seule à me rendre chagrin)

Toujours tel il apparaisse
Entre tes mains sans paresse.

Fan
(of Madame Mallarmé)

WITH nothing for language
But a wingbeat in the skies
The future poem emerges
From its most precious dwelling

Wing in low descent the herald
This fan if this is
The same through which behind
You in some mirror

Translucent (where will redescend
Pursued in each particle
A bit of invisible ash
Sole cause of my sadness)

Always so let it emerge
Between your mobile hands.

Autre Éventail
(de Mademoiselle Mallarmé)

O rêveuse, pour que je plonge
Au pur délice sans chemin,
Sache, par un subtil mensonge,
Garder mon aile dans ta main.

Une fraîcheur de crépuscule
Te vient à chaque battement
Dont le coup prisonnier recule
L'horizon délicatement.

Vertige! voici que frissonne
L'espace comme un grand baiser
Qui, fou de naître pour personne,
Ne peut jaillir ni s'apaiser.

Sens-tu le paradis farouche
Ainsi qu'un rire enseveli
Se couler du coin de ta bouche
Au fond de l'unanime pli!

Le sceptre des rivages roses
Stagnants sur les soirs d'or, ce l'est,
Ce blanc vol fermé que tu poses
Contre le feu d'un bracelet.

Another Fan
(of Mademoiselle Mallarmé)

O dreamer, that I may plunge
Into pure, pathless delight,
Learn, by a subtle illusion,
How to guard my wing in your hand.

A twilight coolness is wafted
Toward you with every wingbeat
Whose prisoned stroke daintily
Pushes the horizon back.

Vertigo! See how space trembles
Like an intense kiss which
Mad to be born in vain
Can neither spring forth nor be still.

Do you feel paradise
Fierce as buried laughter
Flow from the corner of your mouth
Down the unanimous fold?

The sceptre of rose-hued shores
Stagnant on evenings of gold, is
This white furled flight you pose
Against the fire of a bracelet.

Éventail

DE frigides roses pour vivre
Toutes la même interrompront
Avec un blanc calice prompt
Votre souffle devenu givre

Mais que mon battement délivre
La touffe par un choc profond
Cette frigidité se fond
En du rire de fleurir ivre

A jeter le ciel en détail
Voilà comme bon éventail
Tu conviens mieux qu'une fiole

Nul n'enfermant à l'émeri
Sans qu'il y perde ou le viole
L'arôme émané de Méry.

Fan

THE frigid roses in order to exist
All of a kind will still
With a sublime white calyx
Your breath become hoar-frost

But let my fluttering liberate
The tuft by a profound shock
The frigidity will dissolve
Into laughter of blossoming rapture

To hurl the sky into fragments
See how like a fine fan
You serve better than a phial

No one which when sealing it tight
Fails to lose or violate
The aroma issuing from Méry.

Feuillet d'Album

TOUT à coup et comme par jeu
Mademoiselle qui voulûtes
Ouïr se révéler un peu
Le bois de mes diverses flûtes

Il me semble que cet essai
Tenté devant un paysage
A du bon quand je le cessai
Pour vous regarder au visage

Oui ce vain souffle que j'exclus
Jusqu'à la dernière limite
Selon mes quelques doigts perclus
Manque de moyens s'il imite

Votre très naturel et clair
Rire d'enfant qui charme l'air.

Album Leaf

SUDDENLY as in a jest
Mademoiselle who desired
To hear a little how sounds
The wood of my various flutes

It seems that this task
Essayed in the midst of a landscape
Gained value when I paused
To gaze upon your face

Yes, this vain breath which I restrained
To the very last moment
Due to my crippled fingers
Lacks the means to try to match

Your most natural and clear
Child-like laugh which charms the air.

Remémoration d'Amis Belges

A des heures et sans que tel souffle l'émeuve
Toute la vétusté presque couleur encens
Comme furtive d'elle et visible je sens
Que se dévêt pli selon pli la pierre veuve

Flotte ou semble par soi n'apporter une preuve
Sinon d'épandre pour baume antique le temps
Nous immémoriaux quelques-uns si contents
Sur la soudaineté de notre amitié neuve

O très chers rencontrés en le jamais banal
Bruges multipliant l'aube au défunt canal
Avec la promenade éparse de maint cygne

Quand solennellement cette cité m'apprit
Lesquels entre ses fils un autre vol désigne
A prompte irradier ainsi qu'aile l'esprit.

Recollection of Belgian Friends

AT certain hours and with no breeze stirring it
All the antiquated almost the shade of incense
(I sense how the widowed stone secretly and visibly
Unveils herself fold after fold)

Floats or seems to bear no token of itself
Unless it be to shed time's ancient balm
On the suddenness of our so recent friendship
We immemorial so contented few

O dear ones, encountered in the never banal
Bruges multiplying the dawn in the still canal
With its scattered procession of swans

When solemnly the city taught me
Who among her sons traces a different flight
To illumine as it does the wing, the Spirit.

Dame sans trop d'ardeur....

D<small>AME</small>
>   sans trop d'ardeur à la fois enflammant
La rose qui cruelle ou déchirée et lasse
Même du blanc habit de pourpre le délace
Pour ouïr dans sa chair pleurer le diamant

Oui sans ces crises de rosée et gentiment
Ni brise quoique, avec, le ciel orageux passe
Jalouse d'apporter je ne sais quel espace
Au simple jour le jour très vrai du sentiment,

Ne te semble-t-il pas, disons, que chaque année
Dont sur ton front renaît la grâce spontanée
Suffise selon quelque apparence et pour moi

Comme un éventail frais dans la chambre s'étonne
A raviver du peu qu'il faut ici d'émoi
Toute notre native amitié monotone.

Lady without too much of ardor....

LADY
without too much of ardor at a time inflaming
the rose who cruel or rent, and weary
Even of her white robe, unlaces it with deep crimson
To hear in her flesh the diamond weeping

Yes, without those crises of dew, and gently,
Without wind, though with its tempestuous sky passes
Jealous to cause, I know not what clearing
In the simple day, the most true day of feeling

Does it not seem to you, say, that each year
Whose spontaneous grace is reborn on your brow
Suffices for appearance's sake, and for me

As a cool fan in a room is astonished
To revive with what slight flutter is required here
The whole natural monotone of our friendship.

O si chère de loin et proche et blanche....

O si chère de loin et proche et blanche, si
Délicieusement toi, Mary, que je songe
A quelque baume rare émané par mensonge
Sur aucun bouquetier de cristal obscurci

Le sais-tu, oui! pour moi voici des ans, voici
Toujours que ton sourire éblouissant prolonge
La même rose avec son bel été qui plonge
Dans autrefois et puis dans le futur aussi.

Mon cœur qui dans les nuits parfois cherche à s'entendre
Ou de quel dernier mot t'appeler le plus tendre
S'exalte en celui rien que chuchoté de sœur

N'était, très grand trésor et tête si petite,
Que tu m'enseignes bien toute une autre douceur
Tout bas par le baiser seul dans tes cheveux dite.

O so dear from afar and near and white....

O so dear from afar and near and white, so
Delightfully you, Mary, that I imagine
Some rare balsam exuded by deceit
Upon some vase of clouded crystal

Do you know, yes! for me it is years since, it is
Forever that your dazzling smile preserves
The same rose with its lovely summer plunging
Into the past as well as into the future.

My heart which sometimes in the night tries to listen
—Or by what lofty and tender word to address you
Rejoices in that of Sister, even only whispered

Were it not, most precious treasure and head so fine,
That you indeed teach me quite another endearment
Softly proclaimed only by the kiss in your hair.

Rondel I

RIEN au réveil que vous n'ayez
Envisagé de quelque moue
Pire si le rire secoue
Votre aile sur les oreillers

Indifféremment sommeillez
Sans crainte qu'une haleine avoue
Rien au réveil que vous n'ayez
Envisagé de quelque moue

Tous les rêves émerveillés
Quand cette beauté les déjoue
Ne produisent fleur sur la joue
Dans l'œil diamants impayés
Rien au réveil que vous n'ayez.

Rondel I

NOTHING on waking which you had not
Envisaged with some pouting
Worse if laughter shake
Your wing on the pillows

Sleep without concern
With no fear that a breath avows
Anything on waking which you had not
Envisaged with some pouting

All the dreams astonished
When this beauty foils them
Yield not a flower on the cheek
Unpaid diamonds in the eye
Nothing on waking which you had not.

Rondel II

SI tu veux nous nous aimerons
Avec tes lèvres sans le dire
Cette rose ne l'interromps
Qu'à verser un silence pire

Jamais de chants ne lancent prompts
Le scintillement du sourire
Si tu veux nous nous aimerons
Avec tes lèvres sans le dire

Muet muet entre les ronds
Sylphe dans la pourpre d'empire
Un baiser flambant se déchire
Jusqu'aux pointes des ailerons
Si tu veux nous nous aimerons.

Rondel II

IF you wish we will love each other
With your lips without words
Do not cleave this rose
To pour forth a worse silence

Never do songs swiftly spark
The scintillation of a smile
If you wish we will love each other
With your lips without words

Silently silently between the rounds
Sylph in imperial crimson
A flaming kiss is rent apart
Unto the very tips of the pinions
If you wish we will love each other.

Billet à Whistler

PAS les rafales à propos
De rien comme occuper la rue
Sujette au noir vol de chapeaux;
Mais une danseuse apparue

Tourbillon de mousseline ou
Fureur éparses en écumes
Que soulève par son genou
Celle même dont nous vécûmes

Pour tout, hormis lui, rebattu
Spirituelle, ivre, immobile
Foudroyer avec le tutu,
Sans se faire autrement de bile

Sinon rieur que puisse l'air
De sa jupe éventer Whistler.

Note to Whistler

NO gusts of wind to no purpose
But to pervade the street
Exposed to the black flight of hats;
But a dancer appeared

Whirlwind of chiffon or
Fury scattered in foam
Which she for whom we lived
Stirs up with her knee

Witty, intoxicated, motionless
All banality except him,
To blast with her tutu
Without any further worry

Save that the breeze of her skirt
May gaily fan Whistler.

Petit Air I

QUELCONQUE une solitude
Sans le cygne ni le quai
Mire sa désuétude
Au regard que j'abdiquai

Ici de la gloriole
Haute à ne la pas toucher
Dont maint ciel se bariole
Avec les ors de coucher

Mais langoureusement longe
Comme de blanc linge ôté
Tel fugace oiseau si plonge
Exultatrice à côté

Dans l'onde toi devenue
Ta jubilation nue.

Little Air I

JUST any solitude
With neither swan nor quay
Mirrors its desuetude
In the glance I turn

Here from the lofty
Unattainable vainglory
Discordant hues which many a sky
Mixes with golds of sunset

But languorously coasts
Like white linen shed
As a fleeting bird if,
Enraptured beside, dives

Into the wave become you,
Your naked jubilation.

Petit Air II

INDOMPTABLEMENT a dû
Comme mon espoir s'y lance
Eclater là-haut perdu
Avec furie et silence,

Voix étrangère au bosquet
Ou par nul écho suivie,
L'oiseau qu'on n'ouït jamais
Une autre fois en la vie.

Le hagard musicien,
Cela dans le doute expire
Si de mon sein pas du sien
A jailli le sanglot pire

Déchiré va-t-il entier
Rester sur quelque sentier!

Little Air II

INDOMITABLY as
My hope takes wing
Above there, lost, must have
Burst with fury and silence,

A strange voice in the thicket
Which no echo repeated
The bird one may hear
Never again in this life.

The haggard musician,
It expires in doubt
Whether from my breast not his
Surged the deeper sob

Though torn will he be left whole
On some unknown road.

Quand l'ombre menaça de la fatale loi...

QUAND l'ombre menaça de la fatale loi
Tel vieux Rêve, désir et mal de mes vertèbres,
Affligé de périr sous les plafonds funèbres
Il a ployé son aile indubitable en moi.

Luxe, ô salle d'ébène où, pour séduire un roi
Se tordent dans leur mort des guirlandes célèbres,
Vous n'êtes qu'un orgueil menti par les ténèbres
Aux yeux du solitaire ébloui de sa foi.

Oui, je sais qu'au lointain de cette nuit, la Terre
Jette d'un grand éclat l'insolite mystère,
Sous les siècles hideux qui l'obscurcissent moins.

L'espace à soi pareil qu'il s'accroisse ou se nie
Roule dans cet ennui des feux vils pour témoins
Que s'est d'un astre en fête allumé le génie.

When with its fatal law the shadow threatened....

WHEN with its fatal law the shadow threatened
A certain former Dream, desire and ill of my spine,
Distressed at dying beneath funereal ceilings
It folded its fateful wing in me.

Luxury, O ebony hall where to seduce a king
Renowned garlands are writhing in their death,
You are but pride falsified by the dark
In the eyes of the hermit dazzled by his faith.

Yes, I know that in the far distance of this night, the Earth
Casts the wondrous mystery of a great splendor
Among the hideous centuries which darken it less.

Space indifferent to whether it expands or draws in
Rolls in that ennui vile fires as witnesses
That from a festive star a genius was kindled.

Le vierge, le vivace et le bel aujourd'hui....

LE vierge, le vivace et le bel aujourd'hui
Va-t-il nous déchirer avec un coup d'aile ivre
Ce lac dur oublié que hante sous le givre
Le transparent glacier des vols qui n'ont pas fui!

Un cygne d'autrefois se souvient que c'est lui
Magnifique mais qui sans espoir se délivre
Pour n'avoir pas chanté la région où vivre
Quand du stérile hiver a resplendi l'ennui.

Tout son col secouera cette blanche agonie
Par l'espace infligée à l'oiseau qui le nie,
Mais non l'horreur du sol où le plumage est pris.

Fantôme qu'à ce lieu son pur éclat assigne,
Il s'immobilise au songe froid de mépris
Que vêt parmi l'exil inutile le Cygne.

Virginal, vibrant and beautiful today....

WILL virginal, vibrant and beautiful today
Shatter with a blow of its rapturous wing
This solid lost lake where beneath the frost haunts
The transparent glacier of unrealized flights!

A swan of yore recalls he was
Magnificent but from hope delivered
For failing to sing of the realm of life
When from sterile winter glistened ennui.

His whole throat will thrust off this white agony
Inflicted by space on the bird who denied it,
But not the horror of the place where his plumage is trapped.

Phantom whose pure brilliance assigns to this space
He is frozen in the cold dream of scorn
Which clothes the Swan in his futile exile.

Victorieusement fui le suicide beau....

VICTORIEUSEMENT fui le suicide beau
Tison de gloire, sang par écume, or, tempête!
O rire si là-bas une pourpre s'apprête
A ne tendre royal que mon absent tombeau.

Quoi! de tout cet éclat pas même le lambeau
S'attarde, il est minuit, à l'ombre qui nous fête
Excepté qu'un trésor présomptueux de tête
Verse son caressé nonchaloir sans flambeau,

La tienne si toujours le délice! la tienne
Oui seule qui du ciel évanoui retienne
Un peu de puéril triomphe en t'en coiffant

Avec clarté quand sur les coussins tu la poses
Comme un casque guerrier d'impératrice enfant
Dont pour te figurer il tomberait des roses.

Victoriously having renounced the glorious suicide....

VICTORIOUSLY having renounced the glorious suicide
Embers of glory, blood in foam, gold, tempest!
O what a jest if yonder crimson is preparing
To regally drape only my absent tomb.

What! Of all this splendor, not even a shred
Lingers; it is midnight in our festive darkness
Save that a head's arrogant treasure
Pours forth its caressed nonchalance, without outer light,

Yours, ever a delight! Yours, yes
Which alone of the vanished sky retains
A bit of childish vanity you wind in your hair

With its splendor, when placing it upon the pillows
Like a warrior-helmet of a child empress
From which to depict you, roses would be falling.

Ses purs ongles très haut dédiant leur onyx....

SES purs ongles très haut dédiant leur onyx,
L'Angoisse, ce minuit, soutient, lampadophore,
Maint rêve vespéral brûlé par le Phénix
Que ne recueille pas de cinéraire amphore

Sur les crédences, au salon vide: nul ptyx,
Aboli bibelot d'inanité sonore,
(Car le Maître est allé puiser des pleurs au Styx
Avec ce seul objet dont le Néant s'honore).

Mais proche la croisée au nord vacante, un or
Agonise selon peut-être le décor
Des licornes ruant du feu contre une nixe,

Elle, défunte nue en le miroir, encor
Que, dans l'oubli fermé par le cadre, se fixe
De scintillations sitôt le septuor.

Its pure nails offering very high their onyx....

ITS pure nails offering very high their onyx,
Anguish, this midnight, bears, like a candelabra,
Many an evening dream consumed by the Phoenix
Not gathered up in any funeral amphora

On the credenzas, in the empty salon: No seashell,
Vanished curio of sonorous emptiness,
(For the Master has gone to draw tears from the Styx
With this sole object in which the Void takes pride).

But near the window open to the north, a gold
Is dying composing a kind of decor
Of unicorns hurling fire at a nixie,

She, a dead nude in the mirror, although,
In the oblivion enclosed by the frame, at once
The scintillations of The Seven Stars are fixed.

Sonnet

(Pour votre chère morte, son ami)

—« SUR les bois oubliés quand passe l'hiver sombre
Tu te plains, ô captif solitaire du seuil,
Que ce sépulcre à deux qui fera notre orgueil
Hélas! du manque seul des lourds bouquets s'encombre.

Sans écouter Minuit qui jeta son vain nombre,
Une veille t'exalte à ne pas fermer l'œil
Avant que dans les bras de l'ancien fauteuil
Le suprême tison n'ait éclairé mon Ombre.

Qui veut souvent avoir la Visite ne doit
Par trop de fleurs charger la pierre que mon doigt
Soulève avec l'ennui d'une force défunte.

Ame au si clair foyer tremblante de m'asseoir,
Pour revivre il suffit qu'à tes lèvres j'emprunte
Le souffle de mon nom murmuré tout un soir.»

Sonnet
(For your dear dead lady, her friend)

—"WHEN somber winter drifts over the abandoned woods
You lament, O lonely prisoner of the threshold,
That this sepulchre for two which will be our pride
Alas! is laden only with absence of weighty bouquets.

Deaf to Midnight which casts its vain number,
A vigil urges you to remain awake
Until the last ember has illumined my Shade
There enfolded in the old arm-chair.

Who longs for frequent Visitation, must not
Burden with too many flowers the stone which my finger
Lifts with the lassitude of a departed strength.

Soul trembling to be seated at such a bright hearth,
To live again, I need solely from your lips to borrow
The breath of my name murmured all evening long."

Le Tombeau d'Edgar Poe

TEL qu'en Lui-même enfin l'éternité le change,
Le Poète suscite avec un glaive nu
Son siècle épouvanté de n'avoir pas connu
Que la mort triomphait dans cette voix étrange!

Eux, comme un vil sursaut d'hydre oyant jadis l'ange
Donner un sens plus pur aux mots de la tribu
Proclamèrent très haut le sortilège bu
Dans le flot sans honneur de quelque noir mélange.

Du sol et de la nue hostiles, ô grief!
Si notre idée avec ne sculpte un bas-relief
Dont la tombe de Poe éblouissante s'orne,

Calme bloc ici-bas chu d'un désastre obscur,
Que ce granit du moins montre à jamais sa borne
Aux noirs vols du Blasphème épars dans le futur.

The Tomb of Edgar Poe

JUST as eternity transforms him at last unto Himself,
The Poet rouses with a naked sword
His age terrified at not having discerned
That death was triumphant in that strange voice!

They, like a Hydra's vile spasm on hearing the angel
Once give a purer meaning to the words of the tribe
Loudly proclaimed the sorcery drunk
In the dishonored flow of some foul brew.

From hostile soil and cloud, O lament!
If our thought fails to carve a bas-relief
With which to adorn the shining tomb of Poe.

Mute block fallen here below from some dim disaster
Let this granite at least forever be a barrier
To the foul flights of Blasphemy scattered in the future.

Le Tombeau de Charles Baudelaire

LE temple enseveli divulgue par la bouche
Sépulcrale d'égout bavant boue et rubis
Abominablement quelque idole Anubis
Tout le museau flambé comme un aboi farouche

Ou que le gaz récent torde la mèche louche
Essuyeuse on le sait des opprobres subis
Il allume hagard un immortel pubis
Dont le vol selon le réverbère découche

Quel feuillage séché dans les cités sans soir
Votif pourra bénir comme elle se rasseoir
Contre le marbre vainement de Baudelaire

Au voile qui la ceint absente avec frissons
Celle son Ombre même un poison tutélaire
Toujours à respirer si nous en périssons.

The Tomb of Charles Baudelaire

THE buried temple discloses through its sepulchral
Mouth of the sewers drooling mud and rubies
Abominably some idol of Anubis
His whole snout aflame with a ferocious bark

Or when the gas newly lit twists the foul wick
Known effacer of the insults suffered
Haggard it lights up an immortal pubis
Whose flight is set in motion by the street-lamp

What dried foliage in the nightless cities
Votive can bless as his Shade can sit once more
In vain against the marble tomb of Baudelaire

In that shivering veil which clothes his absence
This, his very Shade, a guardian poison
To be always inhaled though it may bring us death.

Tombeau
(de Verlaine)

LE noir roc courroucé que la bise le roule
Ne s'arrêtera ni sous de pieuses mains
Tâtant sa ressemblance avec les maux humains
Comme pour en bénir quelque funeste moule.

Ici presque toujours si le ramier roucoule
Cet immatériel deuil opprime de maints
Nubiles plis l'astre mûri des lendemains
Dont un scintillement argentera la foule.

Qui cherche, parcourant le solitaire bond
Tantôt extérieur de notre vagabond—
Verlaine? Il est caché parmi l'herbe, Verlaine

A ne surprendre que naïvement d'accord
La lèvre sans y boire ou tarir son haleine
Un peu profond ruisseau calomnié la mort.

Tomb
(of Verlaine)

THE black rock indignant that the wind-blast rolls it
Will not be stayed even by pious hands
Probing its likeness to human ills
As if to hallow some of their fatal mould.

Here almost always if the ringdove coos
This immaterial mourning afflicts with masses
Of nubile folds tomorrow's full-blown star
Whose scintillation will stream silver on the crowd.

Who seeks, perusing the solitary leap
So recently existent, of our vagabond—
Verlaine? He is hidden in the grass, Verlaine

Only to discover in childlike accord
The lips without drinking, nor draining his breath
A steam so shallow and maligned, death.

Hommage
(à Richard Wagner)

LE silence déjà funèbre d'une moire
Dispose plus qu'un pli seul sur le mobilier
Que doit un tassement du principal pilier
Précipiter avec le manque de mémoire.

Notre si vieil ébat triomphal du grimoire,
Hieroglyphes dont s'exalte le millier
A propager de l'aile un frisson familier!
Enfouissez-le-moi plutôt dans une armoire.

Du souriant fracas originel haï
Entre elles de clartés maîtresses a jailli
Jusque vers un parvis né pour leur simulacre,

Trompettes tout haut d'or pâmé sur les vélins,
Le dieu Richard Wagner irradiant un sacre
Mal tu par l'encre même en sanglots sibyllins.

Tribute
(to Richard Wagner)

ALREADY funereal, the silence of moire
Settles in more than a single fold on the furniture
Which, along with the absence of memory,
The collapse of the principal pillar will hasten.

Our obsolete triumphal revels with the black book,
Hieroglyphs which thrilled the multitude
To proclaim the familiar wing-flutter!
Rather bury it deep in a closet.

Hated by the mocking original fracas
Among those of masterly brilliance, has emerged
As far as the parvis created for their image,

(Loud trumpets of gold swooning on the vellum)
The god Richard Wagner, raying a consecration
In sibylline sobs, hardly silenced even by the ink.

Hommage
(à Puvis de Chavannes)

TOUTE Aurore même gourde
A crisper un poing obscur
Contre des clairons d'azur
Embouchés par cette sourde

A le pâtre avec la gourde
Jointe au bâton frappant dur
Le long de son pas futur
Tant que la source ample sourde

Par avance ainsi tu vis
O solitaire Puvis
De Chavannes
                    jamais seul

De conduire le temps boire
A la nymphe sans linceul
Que lui découvre ta Gloire.

Tribute
(to Puvis de Chavannes)

EVERY Dawn even too dull
To clench a dark fist
Against the azure clarions
Sounded by this deafmute

Has the shepherd with his gourd
Joined to the staff striking hard
Along the path of his future steps
As long as the abundant well springs forth

Thus in advance you live
O solitary Puvis
De Chavannes
                    never alone

To lead the time to drink
At the nymph without a shroud
Which your Genius reveals to it.

Au seul souci de voyager....

AU seul souci de voyager
Outre une Inde splendide et trouble
—Ce salut soit le messager
Du temps, cap que ta poupe double

Comme sur quelque vergue bas
Plongeante avec la caravelle
Ecumait toujours en ébats
Un oiseau d'annonce nouvelle

Qui criait monotonement
Sans que la barre ne varie
Un inutile gisement
Nuit, désespoir et pierrerie

Par son chant reflété jusqu'au
Sourire du pâle Vasco.

To the sole concern of voyaging....

To the sole concern of voyaging
Beyond a splendid and troubled India
—Let this greeting be the messenger
Of the time, the Cape which your stern rounds

As on some low spar
Dipping with the caravel
Was skimming in frolic
A bird of annunciation

Who screeched monotonously
Without the helm veering
Of a useless ore
Night, despair and precious gems

By his cry reflected in the very
Smile of pale Vasco.

Toute l'âme résumée....

TOUTE l'âme résumée
Quand lente nous l'expirons
Dans plusieurs ronds de fumée
Abolis en autre ronds

. Atteste quelque cigare
Brûlant savamment pour peu
Que la cendre se sépare
De son clair baiser de feu

Ainsi le chœur des romances
A la lèvre vole-t-il
Exclus-en si tu commences
Le réel parce que vil

Le sens trop précis rature
Ta vague littérature.

The whole soul enfurled....

THE whole soul enfurled
When slowly we exhale it
In several rings of smoke
Which vanish into other rings

Attests to some cigar
Burning well as long as
The ash drops away
From its bright kiss of fire

Thus the romantic choir
Flies to the lip
Exclude if you begin
The real for it is vile

The too precise sense erases
Your vague literature.

Tout Orgueil fume-t-il du soir....

TOUT Orgueil fume-t-il du soir,
Torche dans un branle étoufée
Sans que l'immortelle bouffée
Ne puisse à l'abandon surseoir!

La chambre ancienne de l'hoir
De maint riche mais chu trophée
Ne serait pas même chauffée
S'il survenait par le couloir.

Affres du passé nécessaires
Agrippant comme avec des serres
Le sépulcre de désaveu,

Sous un marbre lourd qu'elle isole
Ne s'allume pas d'autre feu
Que la fulgurante console.

Does all Pride turn to smoke at evening....

DOES all Pride turn to smoke at evening,
A torch smothered by shaking
Without the immortal breath
Able to survive abandon!

The former chamber of the Heir, filled
With many a rich fallen trophy
Would not be heated even
Should he return by the corridor.

Fateful agonies of the past
Clutching as with talons
The sepulchre of rejection,

Beneath the heavy marble it isolated,
No other fire is kindled
Save by the flashing console.

Surgi de la croupe et du bond....

SURGI de la croupe et du bond
D'une verrerie éphémère
Sans fleurir la veillée amère
Le col ignoré s'interrompt.

Je crois bien que deux bouches n'ont
Bu, ni son amant ni ma mère,
Jamais à la même Chimère,
Moi, sylphe de ce froid plafond!

Le pur vase d'aucun breuvage
Que l'inexhaustible veuvage
Agonise mais ne consent,

Naïf baiser des plus funèbres!
A rien expirer annonçant
Une rose dans les ténèbres.

Risen from the croup and the leap....

RISEN from the croup and the leap
Of a fragile glass vase
Without flowering, the bitter vigil
The neglected stem, stops short.

I, sylph of the cold ceiling,
I am certain never have two mouths
Drunk of the same Chimera,
Neither my mother nor her lover!

The vase pure of any brew
Save infinite widowhood
Agonizes but does not consent,

Naïve and most dismal kiss!
To breathe forth anything which might proclaim
A rose in the darkness.

Une dentelle s'abolit....

UNE dentelle s'abolit
Dans le doute du Jeu suprême
A n'entr'ouvrir comme un blasphème
Qu'absence éternelle de lit.

Cet unanime blanc conflit
D'une guirlande avec la même,
Enfui contre la vitre blême
Flotte plus qu'il n'ensevelit.

Mais, chez qui du rêve se dore
Tristement dort une mandore
Au creux néant musicien

Telle que vers quelque fenêtre
Selon nul ventre que le sien,
Filial on aurait pu naître.

A lace curtain is made void....

A lace curtain is made void
In doubt that the Supreme Game
May half-reveal like a blasphemy
Only eternal absence of a bed.

This unanimous white conflict
Of one garland with another
In flight toward the pallid pane
Floats rather than enshrouds.

But, in him whom the dream gilds
In sadness reposes a lute
Its hollow, void musician

Such that toward some window
Conforming to no womb but its own,
One might be born as Son.

Quelle soie aux baumes de temps....

QUELLE soie aux baumes de temps
Où la Chimère s'exténue
Vaut la torse et native nue
Que, hors de ton miroir, tu tends!

Les trous de drapeaux méditants
S'exaltent dans notre avenue:
Moi, j'ai ta chevelure nue
Pour enfouir mes yeux contents.

Non! La bouche ne sera sûre
De rien goûter à sa morsure,
S'il ne fait, ton princier amant,

Dans la considérable touffe
Expirer, comme un diamant,
Le cri des Gloires qu'il étouffe.

What silk in the balms of time....

WHAT silk in the balms of time
Wherein the Chimera has sickened
Can compare with the twisting and natural cloud
Of your hair which you proffer when not at your mirror!

The holes of prayerful flags
Are exalted in our street:
As for me, I have your unadorned hair
In which to bury my contented gaze.

No! My mouth will not be sure
Of finding savour in its kiss
Unless he, your princely lover,

Causes to expire, like a diamond
In your illustrious crown,
The cry of Glories he is stifling.

M'introduire dans ton histoire....

M'INTRODUIRE dans ton histoire
C'est en héros effarouché
S'il a du talon nu touché
Quelque gazon de territoire

A des glaciers attentatoire
Je ne sais le naïf péché
Que tu n'auras pas empêché
De rire très haut sa victoire

Dis si je ne suis pas joyeux
Tonnerre et rubis aux moyeux
De voir en l'air que ce feu troue

Avec des royaumes épars
Comme mourir pourpre la roue
Du seul vespéral de mes chars.

To bring myself into your story....

To bring myself into your story
Is as a hero rendered shy
If he has touched with naked heel
Some grassy-patch of territory

Ravisher of glaciers
I know not the artless sin
Which you will not have prevented
From laughing aloud for victory

Say if I am not joyous
Thunder and rubies at the axles
To see in the air pierced by this fire

Amid scattered kingdoms
As if expiring purple the wheel
Of the sole vesperal one of my chariots.

A la nue accablante tu....

A la nue accablante tu
Basse de basalte et de laves
A même les échos esclaves
Par une trompe sans vertu

Quel sépulcral naufrage (tu
Le sais, écume, mais y baves)
Suprême une entre les épaves
Abolit le mât dévêtu

Ou cela que furibond faute
De quelque perdition haute
Tout l'abîme vain éployé

Dans le si blanc cheveu qui traîne
Avarement aura noyé
Le flanc enfant d'une sirène.

Silenced by the oppressive cloud....

SILENCED by the oppressive cloud
Lowering of basalt and lava
With also the slavish echoes
And by a sterile trumpet.

What sepulchral shipwreck (You
Know it, foam, but you drool)
Destroyed the stripped mast
Supreme among flotsam

Or that furious with failing
To cause a supreme perdition
With the whole vain abyss let loose

In the trailing so-white hair
Will niggardly have drowned
The infant-flank of a siren.

Mes bouquins refermés....

MES bouquins refermés sur le nom de Paphos
Il m'amuse d'élire avec le seul génie
Une ruine, par mille écumes bénie
Sous l'hyacinthe, au loin, de ses jours triomphaux

Coure le froid avec ses silences de faux,
Je n'y hululerai pas de vide nénie
Si ce très blanc ébat au ras du sol dénie
A tout site l'honneur du paysage faux.

Ma faim qui d'aucuns fruits ici ne se régale
Trouve en leur docte manque une saveur égale:
Qu'un éclate de chair humain et parfumant!

Le pied sur quelque guivre où notre amour tisonne,
Je pense plus longtemps peut-être éperdument
A l'autre, au sein brûlé d'une antique amazone.

Having closed my books....

HAVING closed my books on the name of Paphos
I enjoy, through sheer fantasy, to conjure
An ancient ruin, blessed by a thousand foams,
Yonder beneath a hyacinth tree, in its days of glory.

Let the cold course in the silence of scythes;
I will not hoot some vain lament
Though this so white frolic skimming the bare land denies
To any site the honor of an unreal landscape.

My hunger which no fruits here have gratified
Finds in that eloquent absence an equal savor:
Though one may burst with flesh, sensuous and fragrant!

My foot on some wyvern where our love fans the flame,
Obsessed, perhaps I ponder longer on the other,
With the seared breast of an ancient Amazon.

Salut

RIEN, cette écume, vierge vers
A ne désigner que la coupe;
Telle loin se noie une troupe
De sirènes mainte à l'envers.

Nous naviguons, ô mes divers
Amis, moi déjà sur la poupe
Vous l'avant fastueux qui coupe
Le flot de foudres et d'hivers;

Une ivresse belle m'engage
Sans craindre même son tangage
De porter debout ce salut

Solitude, récif, étoile
A n'importe ce qui valut
Le blanc souci de notre toile.

Toast

NAUGHT, this foam, virgin verse
To depict only the cup
As in the distance plunges a troupe
Of sirens, many upside down.

We are sailing, O my various
Friends, I already on the stern
You, the sumptuous prow which cuts
The tide of thunderbolts and winters;

A lovely intoxication urges me
Fearless of the pitching
To offer upright this toast

Solitude, reef, star
To whatever was worthy
Of the white concern of our sail.

UN COUP DE DÉS

JAMAIS N'ABOLIRA

LE HASARD

UN COUP DE DÉS

JAMAIS

QUAND BIEN MÊME LANCÉ DANS DES CIRCONSTANCES
ÉTERNELLES

DU FOND D'UN NAUFRAGE

SOIT
    que

            l'Abîme

blanchi
        étale
           furieux
                sous une inclinaison
                    plane désespérément

                            d'aile

                        la sienne

                                    par

avance retombée d'un mal à dresser le vol
et couvrant les jaillissements
coupant au ras les bonds

très à l'intérieur résume

l'ombre enfouie dans la profondeur par cette voile alternative

jusqu'adapter
à l'envergure

sa béante profondeur en tant que la coque

d'un bâtiment

penché de l'un ou l'autre bord

LE MAÎTRE

surgi
inférant

de cette conflagration

que se

comme on menace

l'unique Nombre qui ne peut pas

hésite
cadavre par le bras

plutôt
que de jouer
en maniaque chenu
la partie
au nom des flots

un

naufrage cela

                    hors d'anciens calculs
            où la manœuvre avec l'âge oubliée

                    jadis il empoignait la barre

à ses pieds
            de l'horizon unanime

prépare
      s'agite et mêle
            au poing qui l'étreindrait
un destin et les vents

être un autre

                  Esprit
                        pour le jeter
                              dans la tempête
                        en reployer la division et passer fier

écarté du secret qu'il détient

envahit le chef
coule en barbe soumise

direct de l'homme
            sans nef
                  n'importe
                        où vaine

ancestralement à n'ouvrir pas la main
                              crispée
                    par delà l'inutile tête

        legs en la disparition

                         à quelqu'un
                                   ambigu

              l'ultérieur démon immémorial

ayant
            de contrées nulles
                         induit
    le vieillard vers cette conjonction suprême avec la probabilité

                                  celui
                                    son ombre puérile
    caressée et polie et rendue et lavée
                         assouplie par la vague et soustraite
                         aux durs os perdus entre les ais

                                  né
                                    d'un ébat
    la mer par l'aïeul tentant ou l'aïeul contre la mer
                    une chance oiseuse

                                        Fiançailles
        dont
            le voile d'illusion rejailli leur hantise
            ainsi que le fantôme d'un geste

                              chancellera
                              s'affalera

                                   folie

N'ABOLIRA

COMME SI

Une insinuation

au silence

dans quelque proche

voltige

simple

enroulée avec ironie
      ou
           le mystère
                précipité
                    hurlé

tourbillon d'hilarité et d'horreur

autour du gouffre
                sans le joncher
                      ni fuir

              et en berce le vierge indice

                    COMME SI

plume solitaire éperdue

sauf

que la rencontre ou l'effleure une toque de minuit
et immobilise
au velours chiffonné par un esclaffement sombre

cette blancheur rigide

dérisoire
en opposition au ciel
trop
pour ne pas marquer
exigûment
quiconque

prince amer de l'écueil

s'en coiffe comme de l'héroïque
irrésistible mais contenu
par sa petite raison virile
en foudre

soucieux

      expiatoire et pubère

                muet

La lucide et seigneuriale aigrette
au front invisible
scintille
puis ombrage
une stature mignonne ténébreuse
en sa torsion de sirène

par d'impatientes squames ultimes

rire

    que

        SI

de vertige

debout

    le temps
        de souffleter
bifurquées

      un roc

    faux manoir
        tout de suite
            évaporé en brumes

          qui imposa
            une borne à l'infini

$$C'ÉTAIT$$

issu stellaire

$$CE\ SERAIT$$

pire

    non

        davantage ni moins

            indifféremment mais autant

LE NOMBRE

EXISTÂT-IL
autrement qu'hallucination éparse d'agonie

COMMENÇÂT-IL ET CESSÂT-IL
sourdant que nié et clos quand apparu
enfin
par quelque profusion répandue en rareté
SE CHIFFRÂT-IL

évidence de la somme pour peu qu'une

ILLUMINÂT-IL

LE HASARD

Choit
   la plume
      rythmique suspens du sinistre
                      s'ensevelir
            aux écumes originelles
      naguères d'où sursauta son délire jusqu'à une cime
                      flétrie
         par la neutralité identique du gouffre

RIEN

de la mémorable crise
ou se fût
l'événement

accompli en vue de tout résultat nul
                         humain

                    N'AURA EU LIEU
              une élévation ordinaire verse l'absence

                              QUE LE LIEU
inférieur clapotis quelconque comme pour disperser l'acte vide
                      abruptement qui sinon
                       par son mensonge
                            eût fondé
                          la perdition

       dans ces parages
                    du vague
                      en quoi toute réalité se dissout

EXCEPTÉ
à l'altitude
PEUT-ÊTRE
aussi loin qu'un endroit

fusionne avec au delà

hors l'intérêt
quant à lui signalé
en général
selon telle obliquité par telle déclivité
de feux

vers
ce doit être
le Septentrion aussi Nord

UNE CONSTELLATION

froide d'oublie et de désuétude
pas tant
qu'elle n'énumère
sur quelque surface vacante et supérieure
le heurt successif
sidéralement
d'un compte total en formation

veillant
doutant
roulant
brillant et méditant

avant de s'arrêter
à quelque point dernier qui le sacre

Toute Pensée émet un Coup de Dés

A THROW OF THE DICE

NEVER WILL ABOLISH

CHANCE

A THROW OF THE DICE

NEVER

EVEN WHEN CAST IN ETERNAL CIRCUMSTANCES

AT THE HEART OF A SHIPWRECK

WHETHER
    the

           Abyss

whitened
      slack
          raging
               under an incline
                  desperately soars

                           by its own

                                  wing

beforehand relapsed from wrongly steering the flight
and repressing the outbursts
cleaving the bounds at the root

deep inside weighs

the shadow hidden in the depth by this alternate veil

to adjust
to the spread

its yawning depth as great as the hull

of a ship

careening from side to side

THE MASTER

appeared
    inferring

                from this conflagration

                      which

                  as one threatens

         the one Number which can be

                  hesitates
               cadaver by his arm

rather
      than
         as the old madman
            play the game
        in behalf of the waves
                    one

                direct shipwreck

                    beyond outworn calculations
                where the maneuver with age forgotten

                        once he gripped the helm

at his feet
                of the unanimous horizon

prepares itself
    is tossed and merges
            with the fist which would grip it
destiny and the winds

no other

                    Spirit
                        to hurl it
                                into the tempest
                        to seal the gap and to go proudly

cut off from the secret he withholds

surges over the chief
flows over the submissive graybeard

of the man
            without a ship
                no matter
                        where vainly

ancestrally not to unclench his hand
                                    contracted
                            above the worthless head

        legacy on his disappearance

                        to some
                                        unknown

                    the ulterior immemorial demon

having
            from dead lands
                        led
the aged man toward this supreme conjunction with probability

                                    he
                                        the puerile shadow
caressed and polished and drained and washed
                tamed by the wave and freed
            from the unyielding bones lost among the planks

                                    born
                                            of a frolic
        the sea by the sire enticed or the sire compelling the sea
                        idle fortune

                                                        Betrothal
whose
            veil of illusion rekindled their obsession
            as the ghost of a gesture

                                will falter
                                will plummet

                                    madness

NEVER WILL ABOLISH

AS IF

A simple

in the silence

into an approaching

hovers

innuendo

encoiled with irony
                  or
                            the mystery
                                    hurled
                                            howled

whirlwind of hilarity and horror

over the abyss
                              neither scattering it
                                            nor fleeing

                            and rocks therein the virgin symbol

                                                        AS IF

solitary plume lost

save

that a toque of midnight meets or grazes it
and freezes
to the velvet crumpled by a dull guffaw

this stiffened whiteness

derisive
too much
in opposition to heaven
not to weakly
brand
whosoever

bitter prince of the reef

dons the headdress heroic
invincible but curbed
by his limited human mind
in turmoil

anxious

        atoning and pubescent

                    mute

The lucid and seigneurial aigrette
      on the invisible brow
scintillates
    then conceals
     a frail gloomy stature
in her siren's torsion

with impatient end scales

laugh

      which

            IF

of vertigo

upright

    time
          for beating
forked

       a rock

     false castle
         suddenly
              melted into fog

             which imposed
               a limit on infinity

IT WAS

stellar birth

THIS WOULD BE

no

worse

nor better

but as indifferent as

THE NUMBER

EVEN IF IT EXISTED
other than as a straggling hallucination of agony

EVEN IF IT BEGAN AND EVEN IF IT CEASED
hollow as negation and still born
finally
by some profusion spread with rarity
EVEN IF SUMMED UP

evidence of the sum as small as it is

EVEN IF IT ENLIGHTENED

CHANCE

Falls
> *the plume*
> *rhythmic suspense of the disaster*
> > > *to bury itself*
> > *in the primitive foam*
> *from where lately his delirium surged to a peak*
> > *collapsed*
> *by the indifferent neutrality of the abyss*

NOTHING

of the memorable crisis
or the event
                        might have been

completed with no possible result in view
                              human

                    WILL HAVE TAKEN PLACE
                   an ordinary swell discloses the absence

                                      BUT THE PLACE
any mediocre plashing as if to disperse the empty act
                              abruptly which otherwise
                       by its lie
                                   would have justified
                              the perdition

in these parts
                   of the void
                              in which all reality is dissolved

EXCEPT
in the heights
PERHAPS
at so distant a place

that it fuses with infinity

           above human interest
         as pointed out to him
               in general
by such slant by such slope

               of lights

     toward
       what should be
         the Septentrion or North

              A CONSTELLATION

      cold from neglect and disuse
             yet not so much
           that it does not count
       on some empty and superior plane
         the next collision

                  sidereally
      of a final reckoning in the making

watching
      doubting
         revolving
           blazing and meditating

              before it halts
        at some final point which consecrates it

        All Thought emits a Throw of the Dice

Expositions

Apparition

Apparition London: 1863

Henri Cazalis asked Mallarmé to compose a portrait of a young lady as a gift commemorating Mallarmé's "mystical union" with her. Mallarmé, in a letter, referred to her as his "chaste apparition," stating that a portrait of her would require long meditation, for "only art that is limpid and impeccable is chaste enough to sculpt her religiously."

This work indeed has those qualities. It is no wonder Claude Debussy set it to music!

It was written during a sojourn in London, and perhaps was influenced by Danté Gabriel Rosetti and his PreRaphaelite colleagues.

The atmosphere of their paintings opens the poem: A sorrowful moon, weeping Seraphim with drawn bows, etc. The poet is reveling in that delicious nostalgia of the young romantic, musing on the first kiss he has received from the lovely creature he is addressing. As he thus dreams, eyes "glued to the worn pavement," he looks up and suddenly sees her before him in the golden light of twilight which is haloing her hair, and she is laughing. This evokes a memory of his childhood when he had a vision of his guardian angel, "the fairy in her cap of light," whom he perceived letting "snow down white bouquets of perfumed stars" from her "half-closed hands."

The Jinx

Le Guignon Sens: 1862   Paris: April 1887

This intensely bitter poem has been influenced by Edgar Poe, Charles Baudelaire and Théophile Gautier. It reveals, more explicitly, the agonies Mallarmé suffered.

The major theme concerns the Poet (with a capital P), who is a victim of rejection by his contemporaries, and driven to despair. He is as if cursed with a Jinx who pursues him, and who keeps him from the "glory" (spiritual realm). We recall Pegasus, the Winged Horse of Poetry.

They are whipped by rejection (a foul wind). Their "chiseled grooves" evoke the flagellated Christ.

In spite of having to "gnaw on the bitter golden lemon" (their cruel Ideal), they continue to hope, but in vain! Many expired, often as suicides, unrecognized (passage by night).

As they lie dying, they behold, on the horizon, the Angel of Death.

Those who bow to popular taste and debase their art are applauded and rewarded. Those who refuse are mocked and are called "Clowns," and their lot is grief. Nevertheless, they do not give in, but are innovators of a new consciousness, as Prometheus was.

No one pities them. They seem to be cursed with a Jinx, a demon death-force. Because their work is too innovative and lofty to be comprehended by "the crowd," they are met with hostile mockery. This demon sullies the creation of "the rose" (the enlightening work of art), which could have brought renewed hope and vision to the world.

This monster ("a dwarf skeleton....with a plumed toque") is the false mirror-image of the true poet—the cause of infinite bitterness.

Instead of rebelling, these poets continue to pursue their ideal with pride, but filled with rancor. Those who have prostituted themselves to the wishes of the multitude disdain those who have remained true, their real superiors, and do not recognize that these are as gods. They continue to spit contempt upon them until they utterly destroy their spirit, and all that is left for them is "muttering a prayer to the thunder" (the angry gods), to hang themselves on the lampposts.

Futile Petition

Placet Futile Sens: 1862

This irregular sonnet, which was put to music by Debussy and also by Ravel, is a work as charming as the rococo porcelain Sèvres cup depicted.

The poet laments that he is not the Hebe (deity of youth) as portrayed on the porcelain cup which his adored one raises to her lips, and of whom he is jealous for he is unable to receive the kiss thus bestowed. He praises her exquisite hair which, he says, is as if fashioned by divine "goldsmiths." Her lips are the color of raspberries and her white teeth are like a flock of tamed lambs.

He asks that she appoint him to be the shepherd of this flock, so that he may always be near to enjoy her smiles, for he has noted that she has not freely offered him her favors, but has cast only a "closed glance" upon him.

The poem is replete with the images of rococo paintings: a shepherd playing a flute (a repeated symbol of the poet for Mallarmé), a lapdog, pastilles, and a chiffon-robed Princess.

Here we note the obsession of the poet with a headdress of golden hair.

The Clown Reproved

Le Pitre Chatié Tournon: 1864

An earlier version of this sonnet reveals that it is addressed to the eyes of a beloved.

First quatrain:
Her eyes are like lakes of pure water where the poet might find release from his anguish, for his role in the world has become that of a clown, sullied by public life ("the vile soot of the spotlights"). Here he has been able to escape from that tyranny.

Second quatrain:
He denied "the poor Hamlet" within himself (symbol of the poet) who has the responsibility of healing the ills of the world but whose will-force is lamed. He plunged into this relationship with the one addressed, forgetting his clown's costume, and believed there he'd destroyed all those tombs of his previous life (those death-forces), recapturing that virginal purity and

anonymity of the past.

First tercet:
The sun, joyous symbol of purity, accompanied that transformation.

Second tercet:
Then the poet realized that it was that very "greasepaint," the role of Artist with all of its agony, which was the origin of his art. The pure anonymity, which he had achieved in escaping from the struggle in the world, was a death force, frozen ice, like that of crystallized glaciers.

A Negress possessed by a demon....

Une négresse par le démon secouée.... Tournon: 1865

The sonnet "A Negress" elicited condemnatory editorials when it first appeared, and the title (without Mallarmé's corroboration) was changed to "The Rose Lips" with a comment on the manuscript: "Alarming!"

It is one of Mallarmé's explicitly erotic poems, yet in no way may it be called obscene. Actually, all vulgarity is lifted through the genius of the metaphors.

He describes the lusty, vibrant prostitute, a Negress. The juxtaposition of the pale trembling child and the strong, vibrant woman is skillfully presented. The image of "....that singular mouth/ Pale and pink as a seashell" is startling and raises the poem beyond any vulgarity of which it had been accused.

Windows

Les Fenêtres Sens: London: 1863

On June 3, 1863, in a letter to Cazalis, Mallarmé wrote: "Yes—Here-below has an odor of the kitchen. O my Henri, drink deeply of the Ideal: The happiness of the Here-below is as ignoble as contentment."

The setting is a hospital room. A moribund patient, confined to a hospital bed, disgusted with the rank odors, the bare walls, shuffles to the window to observe the reflection of the twilight on the stones below and to watch the sun setting. He plants a fervent kiss on the panes beyond which are freedom and the open sky. The intoxication of the experience makes him momentarily oblivious of his fatal illness, and, entering a world of imagination, he envisions golden galleys on a lavender horizon, and memories of past loves and adventures return and fill him with tranquility.

Here the metaphor of moribund and poet is clarified. In Part Two, the poet compares himself to such a patient, and expresses his disgust with bourgeois mentality and morality which wallow in mediocrity and sense experience. He escapes into a fantasy of a former Paradise where beauty reigned. This may be found in art, in mysticism—the realm of the spiritual Ideal.

For a moment, he sees himself transfigured as Angel. However, the Here-below envelops him, and prevents his ideal pursuits.

Is there no escape, he asks in despair, even if that be found in death where, should he plunge through the window as a suicide, he may risk losing eternity?

The Flowers

Les Fleurs Tournon: 1864

"Les Fleurs" is one of Mallarmé's exquisite lyrics, which one experiences as music. It is addressed to the Great Mother of Creation (Isis-Sophia-Maria).

Stanza one evokes the purity of primal creation, time of golden avalanches and the original rich flora.

Stanza two unfolds fauve gladioli with their swans' throats (swans symbolizing spiritual beings), the divine laurel (plant of Grecian Heroes) and the vermilion of dawn whose skies evoke the Seraphim.

Stanza three introduces the Fall, time of metamorphosis: The hyacinth, the myrtle, associated with death, and the "cruel rose" (personification of Herodias, who plotted the beheading of John the Baptist).

Stanza four presents her juxtaposition—the lily (who is associated with the weeping and suffering Maria). The gold and vermilion have transformed to seas of sighs, blue incense and pale horizons and a weeping moon—an evocation of the Crucifixion.

Stanza five takes a new direction: The poet praises the cithern and the censers, associated with religious ritual. In spite of being bound in the limbos of our "ennui," we send up "Hosannahs" in recognition of such celestial beauty, says the poet.

Stanza six presents us with a sudden shock: The exquisite creations of the Great Mother also contain poison which the despairing poet may imbibe to kill himself.

Renewal

Renouveau Sens: 1862

It is Spring, and after a winter of lucidity, the poet is filled with a sickly sterility. He experiences no color nor inspiration, and has the sensation of an iron ring encircling his head. Sorrowfully, he makes an effort to continue his pursuit of the Ideal which seems now undefined, while outer Nature, in contrast, is in blossom.

He sinks to the ground, "gnawing the warm earth," desperately trying to engrave within it a seed which will sprout. Then, totally exhausted, he lies waiting for the "ennui to lift."

Beyond, the impenetrable sky seems to mock him. Suddenly he hears the birds joyfully chirping, celebrating the Spring, and that ending implies hope.

Anguish

Angoisse Tournon: February 1864

The poet has sought a prostitute, not for physical

satisfaction, but to escape his "fatal ennui."

He expresses the desire to feel no remorse for this act, the same kind he attributes to her in her pauses.

"You who know more of the void than the dead" is a powerful line, connoting the wisdom she must have gathered in the practice of her profession and its encounters.

Although he is filled with noble ideals, he recognizes the dark side of his nature, and that the end of vice is sterility. Thus, filled with utmost despair, frustration and fear, he flees.

Weary of the bitter repose....

Las de l'amer repos.... Tournon: 1864

In a mood of depression, invaded by indolence, the poet feels unworthy of his former ideals and of the task which he once set for himself, one requiring giant effort and renunciation of usual pleasures; and weary of his painful struggle to overcome this sterility, he still dreams of flowering poems, but experiences only the abyss where (without sunlight) only livid ghost-like flowers (creations) bloom.

He longs to escape from the cruel world of the present where he has been maligned and rejected by his contemporaries, and also from the futile vigil at his "lamp" where he spent sleepless nights attempting to create. He longs to return to a previous exotic era when Chinese painters did not portray subjective passionate experiences, but comprehended essence, objectivity, silence, white spaces, and the emptiness which permits the spirit to enter; they used delicate evocative sparse imagery which achieved a transparency through which the spirit might be experienced. This "unsullied ecstasy" was like the unsullied dream of childhood.

This way, in his poems, he would, as on a porcelain cup with suggestive spare color and line, evoke universal essence beyond the physical image.

The Bell Ringer

Le Sonneur Sens: 1862

In this sonnet, the poet compares himself to the bell ringer of a church, who stumbles in exhaustion, with barely the strength to lift the stone which will cause the bell to resound.

Being too close to the bell, he will not hear the clear voice which may be the igniter of a spiritual inspiration in others. In the same way, the poet is unable to experience the effect of his creations, wherein he has striven to set forth his vision of the Ideal in order to thereby illumine and awaken the world still steeped in unconsciousness. It may be that no one listens. The Philistine attitude continues as a death-force.

Depressed by that, his voice no longer resonates, and in the despair engendered by his futile effort, all he is able to do is to envisage his own self-annihilation.

Summer Sadness

Tristesse d'Été Tournon: 1864

This sonnet was addressed to Mallarmé's wife.

On a summer afternoon, they have been lying on the sand, making love. There has been no consummation, and the woman lies asleep while the hot sun in her loosened blond hair and on her cheek causes them to emit a heady fragrance. His kisses were not passionate, and tearfully she declared that she and he would never be as one.

We note again Mallarmé's obsession with golden tresses. He says that it is enough for him to drown his obsessed soul in her hair, that he is able to appreciate a reality in a way which she is unable to understand. Perhaps the mascara mingling with her tears, which he will "taste," will help him achieve the indifference of the distant dispassionate azure and the insensitive stones.

The Azure

L'Azur Tournon: 1864

The blue sky (The Azure) hides the unattainable Ideal. Its infinite beauty mocks the poet who, eternally agonizing with paralyzing sterility, is impotent to attain to it.

Yet, escape from awareness of its omnipresence is impossible.

He calls on the spiritual pollution of the "here-below," that death-force, to approach and to hide (with its deadly veil) that obsessive Azure. He implores his "ennui" to rise and rid him of his paralyzing lethargy, and to take with it the "mire and the pale reeds" (his obstacles to achieved poems). He calls on the pollution of the city to pour so much soot across the blue that the sun is blotted out.

For a moment, he feels liberated from his obsession, and he contemplates joining the mass of Philistines who wallow in materialistic sense experience, for to escape from his agonizing strivings for the Ideal, he will join the contented, unconscious "herd" and await an obscure death.

However, his wish is "in vain," for suddenly he hears the resonating bells of the Angelus which reopen the scar of his obsessive search for the Ideal which he knows to be the ultimate reality. The resonating tones traverse the concealing fogs, and, like a sword which strikes home, pierce him to the core. "There is no escape," he cries out as one haunted: "The Azure! The Azure!...."

In a letter to Cazalis of March 1864, Mallarmé wrote:

"....I worked on it these last days, and I will not hide from you that it gave me an infinite amount of trouble, beside the fact that before taking up the pen, in order to achieve a moment of perfect lucidity, I had to vanquish my harrowing impotence....

"....I do not appear in the first stanza. The Azure torments the impotent in general. In the second, I begin to doubt that I suffer from this cruel illness because of my flight before the pervasive sky. I prepare....by a blasphemous bragging, 'And what haggard night,' the strange idea of evoking the fogs. The prayer to this 'dear ennui' confirms my impotence. In the third stanza I am wild, like the man who sees his implacable desire succeed. The fourth begins by a grotesque exclamation of a schoolboy freed—'the sky is dead!' And immediately, strengthened by that admirable certitude, I implore Matter....

"Weary of the illness which torments me, I desire to taste the common contentment of the crowd, and await an obscure death.... But the enemy is a spectre; the dead sky returns, and I hear who is singing in the blue bells. He passes by indolently and a victor, without being soiled by this fog; he simply transpierces me, at which, full of pride and not seeing therein a just punishment for my cowardice, I cry out that I have an 'immense agony.' Once again I wish to escape, but I feel my error, and avow that 'I am haunted.' I needed all that poignant revelation to motivate the sincere and bizarre cry at the end, 'The Azure.'"

Sea Breeze

Brise Marine Tournon: May 1865

"Sea Breeze" is a fervent expression of Mallarmé's longing to escape from the banality of his monotonous existence, and to set sail for an exotic land where his soul may be inspired and elevated to noble creativity.

Nothing is able to still his restlessness: Neither the ancient gardens of his environment, nor even his young wife nursing their child. He imagines that the excitement of departure will lift his unbearable ennui.

Yet, he thinks the ship may encounter dangers—gales which may cause it to founder far from any shore, that the fertile isles of his dream will prove illusory.

No matter! The "sailor's song" lures him forward for the Journey.

Sigh

Soupir Tournon: 1864

In a letter to Madame Le Josne of February 8, 1868, sent with a copy of "Soupir," Mallarmé referred to the poem as "an autumnal reverie."

This lyric also was set to music by Claude Debussy and Maurice Ravel.

The mood depicts an autumn nostalgia. The poem is addressed to an adored woman, perhaps Marie Gerhard, with whom he'd fallen in love. The poet says that her brow and her eyes mirror an autumnal reflective mood toward which, as he observes her, his soul ascends in the same way that one might experience a garden filled with autumnal melancholy.

As the white jet of the fountain seems to continue to reach upward toward the Azure, with no hope of ever attaining it, so he reaches toward her, yet not in stormy desperation, but as one might experience a soft and pure October day, when on the still lakes dead and fauve colored leaves are moved along by a soft wind, no longer lit by the golden ray of summer, but by a last lingering yellow ray of autumn.

Note the autumn colors depicted in this short lyric: russet, white, azure, fauve, yellow.

The white jet of the fountain suggests his pure feelings toward her, pure as she herself remains.

Alms

Aumône Sens: 1862 Paris: 1887 (Reworked)

A beggar is being addressed by someone offering him a purse, and advising him to spend it indulging some "sin, bizarre and vast."

The tavern where all sins are committed—drugs, luxurious clothes, sex—with the ascending tobacco smoke, creates the false illusion of a church, and here the inhabitants worship at a false shrine of materialism—in other words, the devil. "Do you wish to take part in this life of the lower passions?" the speaker asks.

Now he calls the beggar an "old god," who nevertheless will still leave at dawn wearing his old rags, who will note the beauty of the dawn sky, and whose intoxication will be twofold.

He advises him not to focus on the material, but to stand upright as a hero might stand, and to make an offering at compline to a Saint whom he might still revere. This advice may seem mad, but it is not.

He advises him, above all, not to spend this alms for some material necessity.

And now the metaphor:

Either the speaker is someone who has praised the work of the poet while others have demeaned him, or it is Mallarmé addressing some other rejected poet.

In any case, he assures the other that the praise was sincere, and not a result of wheedling of the desperate poet. He is called a "senile nursling,"—a child in his continued faith, but aged and driven mad with suffering.

He advises the poet to enjoy the offering, to let it inspire him to some bizarre unconventionality. The giver implies that worldly success has led to debasement, that those who achieve what they have bought with mediocrity and deceit worship an illusion which they take for something precious and spend their time reveling in earthly sins. They do not experience the true "nymphs and veils," only false imitations.

From time to time, they toss a bit of recognition to the true but neglected poet who observes them from behind a window—he who is really sublime, yet shivering in his misery. Still, he is able to remain "upright," the artist with his plumed toque (Hamlet), and to make an offering to the Spirit in whom he still has faith (his Ideal). This implies that the others are the truly lost souls.

The giver says that his advice is not mad, for he himself knows the futility of that life.

The last line, solitary, emphatic, advises: Do not use this offering for some banality of the "here-below," but as an inspiration for something "beyond."

Symbols:
Note the ingenious rhyme scheme: terza rima:

a	b	c	d	e	f	g	h
b	c	d	e	f	g	h	i
a	b	c	d	e	f	g	h

The solitary last line rhymes with the i of the last tercet.

Gift of the Poem

Don du Poème Tournon: 1865

In a letter to Madame Le Josne of February 8, 1866, Mallarmé wrote:

"....['Don du Poème'] evokes the sadness of the poet before the Child of his Night, the poem of his....night of sleeplessness, when the wicked dawn revealed it as funereal and lifeless: He brings it to his wife who will revive it...."

The poem is addressed to his wife to whom he offers the "child of an Idumaean night." Idumée was a name hated by the Chosen People and the Prophets—a name of misfortune. It was reputed to be a place where the Kings were able to give birth without women, and bore monsters.

Thus the child or poem which he offers is such a monster—detested, destined for destruction.

The poet has been awake all night agonizing over his creation (birth pangs). The rising dawn is entering through the frozen panes, raying onto the lamp where he has kept his agonizing vigil. The still-lighted lamp is in the form of an Angel. Now in the rays of light, which are designated as "Palms" which also invoke Idumée, he, the father of the poem, observes his "child," and sees it as a lifeless, bleeding monster with featherless wings, meaning it will never be capable of soaring. Only a hostile smile can welcome it into the world. Once again, he experiences his sterility and his solitude. He addresses his wife who, perhaps in a nearby room, is cradling her and his natural child, and he offers her this "ghastly birth," for she is tender, pure and filled with reverent beauty (like the Madonna), and he asks her to bless this child (and also himself, the poet) with her pure, nourishing love and inspiration, for he is starved by his inability to realize the Ideal creation.

Canticle of Saint John

Cantique de Saint Jean Tournon: 1864

"Cantique de Saint Jean" is an excerpt from Mallarmé's long

dramatic work "Hérodiade." It is a unique poem, composed in four foot hexameter verse.

When the Sun, at its zenith point and about to begin its descent along the zodiacal circle, seems to halt for an infinitesimal instant, the severed head ascending seems to parallel the Sun in that pause.

The scythe itself is like a wing in triumphal flight, and also it symbolizes Death which has made that triumph possible, for the head now is able to behold the Absolute from a heightened point of view, even to that cold eternal void which surpasses the height of glaciers, there to be beatified. The rupture caused by the decapitation may at last put an end to the archetypal discord between the head (Mind, Spirit) and the flesh (Matter).

But as Saint John was consecrated by the Divine Christ at the Baptism, who Himself leaned down in love toward the Earth, this head, now descending, also may serve the Earth on a spiritual level.

Her mass of hair....

La chevelure.... Paris: 1887

Chevelure means not only tresses of hair, but also those of a comet, trailing its flame across the dark sky. The title itself, therefore, excites expectation.

The poem is in the form of an English sonnet, composed of three quatrains and a distique, and is considered technically perfect.

The poet observes his mistress with her golden hair plaited in the convention of the era, sedately contained. He imagines it unfurled, loosened and streaming toward the West, which here represents the place of desires and passion.

Plaited, it rests on her forehead like a diadem, an image which evokes the Virgin, the Madonna. Yet, her eyes hold an inner fire which flashes and contradicts the sedate impression such a hairstyle might suggest.

Although her gestures negate any hint of seduction, the poet doubts the value of this contained passion when her hair, loosened and flowing, would reveal her splendor. Yet, in the manner in which she holds her head and the halo-like radiance her hair emits, he recognizes her pride and dignity.

On another level, we may recognize this as a metaphor connected with poetic art. True art must suppress the subjective sensual, yet retain an inner fire, and, like the light of a torch, scatter rubies into the dark—that is, new vibrant vision.

Hair is a recurring symbol of Mallarmé. In his poem "Apparition," there is the "fairy with her cap of brightness." In "Anguish": "In your tresses' impurity, a dismal storm." In "Hérodiade," the red mass of her hair becomes a significant symbol. In "Victoriously fled....," golden hair is associated with the sunset. In "What silk in the balms of time....," hair is compared to a silk flag, and in "Chevelure," the hair becomes a torch.

Saint

Sainte Tournon: 1865

The original title of this exquisite sonnet was "Saint Cecilia Playing on the Wing of a Cherubim."

Composed of one sentence divided by a semicolon, it becomes a diptych.

Saint Cecilia, Saint of Music, is depicted near a window whose ledge conceals the ancient sandalwood lute, which once having shone with the ancient flute and mandore, now has its gilt peeling.

The pale Saint is displaying an ancient missal, open at the *Magnificat* for the service of vespers or compline.

Another kind of window, on a more spiritual level, reveals the Monstrance, the Holy Chalice, while nearby an Angel is poised for evening flight, the spread wing of her plumage resembling a harp. The delicate fingertip of the Saint is raised as if she is about to play this instrumental plumage, as perhaps the Poet holds the pen poised above the sheet, but her finger touches neither the book nor the instrument, symbols of poetry and music, the music of silence—a celestial, not terrestrial, music of the realm of the Universals toward which all music and poetry aspire.

Funeral Toast

Toast Funèbre Paris: 1875

In his bibliography of 1898, Mallarmé states that "Toast Funèbre" is addressed to Gautier and results from the composite work "The Tomb of Théophile Gautier, Master and Shade."

In 1869, Mallarmé was plunged into a personal crisis, out of which he emerged with new poetic inspiration. His letters reveal that he had descended into a spiritual and intellectual inferno, rejecting all belief in immortality and resurrection. This poem brought him out of his creative sterility, and he concluded that Art alone was justification of human existence.

Section one:

The poem takes place at the tomb of Gautier where Mallarmé is to give the libation and elegy. The poet raises his cup adorned with a golden monster, a chalice which has some connection with St. John; but this is a pale gesture and also madness (folie), for belief in immortality is an illusion. To believe that death is a passage to another life is a vain hope. Perhaps all that remains of him is contained in the tomb. Yet, a new creed is proclaimed: A poet having practiced the ardent career of poetry will not be mere ashes of the common herd, but a hero, a window reflecting the evening sunlight. His creation, now part of the human heritage, serves as an influence and lives on among the lighthouse beacons.

Section two:

Three adjectives open this passage (magnificent, total, solitary), signifying that Gautier achieved glory, fulfillment, his Spirit Self. He has now become like a God.

Mallarmé scorns sentimentality (the lucid horror of a tear). Gautier's pride is in contrast to that of the "haggard crowd"—cowardly and false—incapable of facing death with nobility and courage.

Perhaps in this crowd of opaque phantoms, there is one, "a passerby," listening (Mallarmé once referred to Rimbaud as "a considerable passerby")—who had been blind and mute, but who now, through the inspiration of Gautier, may become the new "virgin hero" (pure Poet).

The vast abyss of the Void rushes toward this newly dead man, Gautier, to ask him to explain the meaning of the Earth once cherished, from which he has departed, and an exhausted voice answers, "I know not."

Section three:

Fear of the Void and Death have now been dispelled. The Master (Gautier) wanders about the gardens of the world ("Eden"—primal Nature) with deeper perception than others. The Poet's eye fixes upon those flowers which it singles out (the rose and the lily), and brings them rain and diamond light, the nourishment they crave—that is, identity which may immortalize them by exalting them to the plane of everlasting art and spirit. Such acts of creative cognition survive the body's death. Genius does not vanish. His words, like wings, take flight into the world, and help the world survive physical death. The artist who brings balance out of chaos is exalted. The death of Gautier is like that meteoric "disaster" which purifies the Earth's atmosphere.

Last section:

The authentic groves are there, where Nature has been transfigured by Art. The true Poet watches over them, denying them a false religious sentimentality, and now, the morning after his death which has silenced him physically, he will transcend the sepulchre which contains only the decaying corpse and the vast night. The poet lives on beyond the mortal existence, transfigured, for his words have altered world destiny.

Prose
(for des Esseintes)

Prose (pour des Esseintes) Paris: 1884

"Prose" was written in response to a letter from Joris Karl Huysmans in 1882 wherein he asks Mallarmé for some poetry to be included in his novel *Against the Grain*, in which des Esseintes is a character. This poem, "Hérodiade" and "L'Après midi d'un faune" called forth the first serious attention to the work of Mallarmé.

"Prose," or *Prosae*, were religious works written in decadent Latin in which rhymes appear for the first time in the language. The octosyllabic lines resemble the technique of early Christian liturgy. The poem is crafted like a well-polished jewel.

"Hyperbole," a metaphor, here symbolizes the supreme flight of the imagination.

The poet asks:

"Imagination, do you no longer rise triumphantly from my memory when I write poetry, for now you have become a product of technique, imprisoned in a kind of tomb—a 'grimoire' with a cover of iron.

"You have become intellectual, abstract, a 'labor of patience'; a mere map, not a garden, but a herbarium.

"Once, my sister and I wandered amid Nature, innocently and instantaneously experiencing its beauty.

"However, the Age of Reason has given everything an arbitrary name, and does not accept our insight that the sunlit flowered garden has its reality beyond the representational, within the Idea, the Ideal, the Universal." (Poetry should be evocative, depicting the Ideal, not the physical landscape.)

"The noon of a hundred irises cannot be located on any map, but in the realm of true imagination. There we could experience grandiose flowers, not of any material realm, and we had no need to analyze that experience. Each flower became individualized, encircled with a corona of light which separated it from the anonymity of the mass." (Implied is that the poem also, each word illumined, must reveal reality beyond.)

"That insight corroborated and manifested what I had longed for and divined."

But the companion, sister, merely smiles as if to say, "Give up that paradisiacal vision." She "abdicates her ecstasy," and pronounces the word "Anastasius!" (which implies resurrection).

She recalls him to the present and his task: Present consciousness requires definition. He must be the poet of refined techniques, using the word to define experience for the evolution of human consciousness. Losing oneself in the mystical can lead to madness.

But resurrection implies a death, and indeed there is a sepulchre in "some unknown clime," on which is engraved the name "Pulcheria!" (Beauty). That tomb is poetry in which Beauty is interred.

Thus, blending Anastasius with "Pulcheria" will heal the split between brother and sister—the eternal feminine and masculine. The poet now realizes the necessity to embody the Universal in the Word in such a way that the rigidification of the merely abstract and the dissolution of the merely mystical, two death forces, are overcome. However, even the imaginative must be overcome. The artifice of art is like a too grand lily which can hide Beauty. One must so create that the Idea, the Concept, and the realm beyond the concept—the Universal—are made manifest. It is buried as soon as it enters cold reality, yet Art may be the instrument of sister's resurrection, which assures her a periodic relative definition.

Fan
(of Madame Mallarmé)

Éventail (de Madame Mallarmé) Paris: March 1891

The original was written in red ink on a paper fan, decorated with white daisies.

The poem emerges into the word (language) with a mere flutter as a butterfly emerges from a chrysalis.

This fan, which the owner holds low and flutters, is a kind of herald of a creative act, and it is reflected in a mirror located behind her.

It becomes the symbol of the poem—the cognitive act—which is first a reflection of the image on the "memory mirror-shield" within, before breaking through to the concept—the Idea.

Every wingbeat carries a "feather of flying ash"—a process of materializations of individual facets of an object, which finally will lead to their dissolution and the revelation of the "flame," or Universal. The words are like the ashes—but necessary so that the "flame" may be revealed on a higher reality.

The beating of the fan is like the annunciation of the poem which is experienced as a "wingbeat" to prepare the flight.

The poet expresses the hope that she will always thus symbolize his inspiration.

Another Fan
(of Mademoiselle Mallarmé)

Autre Éventail (de Mademoiselle Mallarmé) Paris: 1884

"Another Fan" is addressed to Mallarmé's daughter Geneviève, who was then a twenty year old blond whose portrait in gray and rose was painted by Whistler. This poem also was set to music by Claude Debussy.

The poet addresses the young woman as "dreamer," indicating her youthful unworldliness. It is a warm summer twilight. She is holding a fan which, by the poet's whimsy, he identifies with his "wing."

As she sets the fan in motion, a curve is created which opens the horizon to renewed vision and possibility. This is a recurring Mallarméan symbol of the fan-wing whose trembling brings on that vertigo to creativity.

"Vertigo!" The very space mirrors the restrained kiss on the girl's lips which she does not dare to fulfill.

When he asks if she experiences "paradise," there may be a reference to Eve who begins her temptation of Adam with such a smile, born from "buried laughter," a smile which begins at the corner of her mouth and moves along her closed lips.

Her fan now is compared to a queen's sceptre, rose-hued strands on gold, mirroring the twilight summer sky, now furled—"white-furled flight," indicating innocent virginity, contrasted and contradicted by the fire of her ruby or garnet bracelet.

❖

Fan

Éventail Paris: 1890

"Eventail" was addressed to Méry Laurent, written in white ink on gold paper on a fan imprinted with blossoming roses.

As the fan is set in motion, the roses seem to come alive. Her seeming coldness ("breath become hoar-frost") suddenly dissolves into intoxicating laughter, while the movement of the fan seems also to shatter the sky.

Thus, the fan is more effective than intoxicating liqueur in bringing about that euphoria, since it never need be closed like a bottle of wine whose cork might imprison its flavor. The fan, on the other hand, liberates the scent. Méry herself is like a fine fan who exudes her particular perfume.

Obviously, there is a double erotic nuance in this poem, for here the fan becomes a double erotic symbol.

Album Leaf

Feuillet d'Album Paris: 1890

Mallarmé wrote this poem in the album of Mlle. Roumanville, the daughter of a poet-friend, whom he had admired. It may be she had asked him to recite some verses, which he refers to as the resounding of the wood of his "various flutes." He says that when he paused to look up at her, he knew that his verses could never compare with her natural, charming and child-like beauty, qualities which he has lost. (There may also be an erotic nuance in the poem.)

Recollection of Belgian Friends

Remémoration d'Amis Belges Paris: 1890

In February 1890, Mallarmé had presented a lecture at the

Cercle Excelsior in Bruges, and had met many sympathetic friends.

He recalls how a gray morning mist had draped the antiquated buildings. Incense, which the city itself seems to exude, evokes an atmosphere of reverence which is healing and uplifting.

The widowed stone unveiling herself as the dawn lifts and the sun is beginning to make its appearance recalls the Goddess Isis, known as "The Widow," whose veils, one by one, fall as the sun (Osiris) rises and as the seekers after the Ideal come together. Thus, the image of Bruges casting aside her veils of mist has the deeper nuance of the "veils" being drawn aside to reveal a more lofty consciousness. He feels that he and these fellow artists have been friends eternally. The ebbing currents of the water in the Canal reflect the metamorphosing hues in the sky as the dawn ascends ("....never banal/ Bruges, multiplying the dawn"). Swans glide by, always a symbol of spiritual reality, and the appearance of friends with the same lofty vision as his own has revealed to him those among the Belgians who strive for the spiritual Ideal.

❖

Lady without too much of ardor....

Dame sans trop d'ardeur.... Paris: January 1887

This sonnet, addressed to Méry Laurent on the anniversary of their long relationship, speaks of the continued platonic nature of their friendship which has been "without too much of ardor."

He implies that perhaps she had restrained her inner passion for the sake of society, and it may have transformed to "the diamond weeping....in her flesh."

Yet, that also is precious, and although a "tempestuous sky" did hover with the possibility of a breach in that restrained passion, the present state of their friendship is filled with genuine feeling and true tenderness. With each passing year, her grace has not diminished, and this anniversary is like the gentle agitation of a fan which brings fresh air into a room and announces the tranquil state of their friendship, free of the violence, passion and jealousies elicited by more "ardent" attachments which might have destroyed it.

O so dear from afar and near and white....

O si chère de loin et proche et blanche.... Paris: ~1886

In this sonnet, the poet speaks to a vision of Méry Laurent of the delicate nature of their love.

First quatrain:
Even in absence, he seems to inhale her particular fragrance—a kind of balsam exuded from the rim of a dark crystal.

Second quatrain:
Time has not destroyed her dazzling smile which is like the vase which preserves an eternally unfaded rose.

First tercet:
He rejoices that their wonderful relationship remains ideal—wherein he may address her not as Lover, but as "Sister"—a term both lofty and tender, and which denotes her as equal.

Second tercet:
Yet, when he kisses her hair, something more erotic than aesthetic loftiness is present in his emotion.

Rondel I

Rondel I Paris: 1889

This light poem is addressed to Méry Laurent.

The beloved awakes, perhaps from a disturbing dream, and wondering whether she may have revealed something in her sleep or done something she regrets, she expresses some annoyance. Were her pouting to change to a laugh, the poet would find it more cruel.

He tells her to sleep without concern that anything has occurred which might cause her displeasure.

Her lovely face and brilliant eyes have not in any way been spoiled by any bad dreams or occurrences.

Rondel II

Rondel II Paris: 1889

The poem is addressed to Méry Laurent.

A silent kiss is described without words of love accompanying it. The poet implores her not to interrupt the kiss ("cleave the rose") for perhaps the ensuing silence would indicate something he would not wish to know.

The essential kiss is hidden between the joined lips like a royal sylph in a robe of crimson (the lips). Suddenly the smile, which spreads toward the corners of the lips like the tips of the wings of a cherubim, rends the flaming kiss.

Even here, a superficial kiss is not in question, but the flame of the heightened reality is not in the physical lips but between the joined mouths—there the flame is present.

The smile also has a sudden implication of mockery—which might destroy the ecstasy.

Note to Whistler

Billet à Whistler Paris: November 1890

The poem refers to an English periodical, *The Whirlwind*, which was planned to restore favor on the question of the rehabilitation of the Stuarts. Also, the editors wished to familiarize the English with the work of Mallarmé and to celebrate the paintings of Whistler.

Mallarmé addressed this note to Whistler who expressed much appreciation for it.

Mallarmé implies that the stormy "whirlwind" here does not refer to the usual destructive gossip of satiric journals existent (a wind to blow a hat down a street) but rather will be like the whirlwind dance, a ballet, the ideal of the artist (for "....she for whom we lived...."). (Mallarmé wrote in an essay that the dance in motion is equated with the poet who, through the movement of his thought, destroys the static and rises to a higher stage of consciousness.)

The aim of this new magazine is to shatter banality, but not in anger, not thereby destroying Whistler himself. He tells the painter that he will reap joy from this effort.

Little Air I

Petit Air I Paris: 1891

First quatrain:

It is sunset. The poet is near a river (perhaps the Seine near where Mallarmé once resided). Mirrored in the state of his mind, the scene seems filled with monotony. There is neither a lofty beautiful spirit (swan), nor a counterpoint of pause and refuge (quay).

Second quatrain:

The sky, sunset-hued and mingled with gold, seems unattainable (as is the vainglory of the poet).

Third quatrain: Last couplet:

A white bird skims across the sky. Simultaneously, a woman has appeared who, discarding her white linen robe, dives into the water, mirroring the bird. Graceful, carefree, she dives into the wave, becomes the wave, thus shattering the wave's unanimity, "the ennui."

Implied is that the poet also must shed his white shroud of sterility and ennui, and with his will force, dive into the act of creativity, thus becoming his own "jubilation."

Little Air II

Petit Air II Paris: 1891

This sonnet of despair challenges the often repeated charge that Mallarmé's poems are too cerebral and without feeling.

First quatrain:
A strange furious song of a bird is heard in the forest, followed by silence.

Second quatrain:
The voice, unusual and strange, is echoless. Nothing of its song will remain. It is as "strange" as the poet's own voice and will be totally forgotten.

Third quatrain:
The bird is a "haggard singer," as the poet is a "haggard musician," its cry of despair paralleling the profound sob in the breast of the poet.

Last couplet:
Some violent force, perhaps, has destroyed the bird who will lie smashed on an anonymous pavement, mourned by no one, as the poet himself has been destroyed by rejection. Thus, he also may lie shattered "on a pavement"—an anonymous suicide, silenced and forgotten.

When with its fatal law the shadow threatened....

Quand l'ombre menaça de la fatale loi.... Paris: 1883

First quatrain:
The "fatal law" is the inevitable death sentence under which the earthly being is fated at birth, and already it presages the destruction of one's dream of immortality and of his passionate desire, which, although grand, also was the cause of

his anguish. Death is here seen as a dark bird.

Second quatrain:
Under the night sky, the earth resembles a luxurious death chamber. It is like an "ebony Hall" wherein Kings felt themselves to be immortal. Here the "renowned garlands" are the stars which seem like living beings because one believed them to be divine, but actually they are dead bodies, creating false illusions of glory.

First tercet:
Nevertheless, there *is* a great splendor in the mystery of the heavens which, though unfathomable, cannot be effaced even by the horrors of history.

Second tercet:
"Space" is indifferent to our conjectures concerning it, and yet, in that seeming monotonous "ennui," those stars ("vile fires") are as witnesses of that particular constellation (the Universal or "Notion," as Hegel calls it) which is said, esoterically, to give birth to and to sustain genius. Thus, beyond the despair and cynicism of the initial thoughts, that constellation represents a hope that a mysterious, unfathomable divinity is revealed existing beyond the knowable through whom great artists are sent as messengers to humankind.

Virginal, vibrant and beautiful today....

Le vierge, le vivace, et le bel aujourd'hui....   Paris: 1885

In exquisite imagery, this poem expresses the sterility, impotence and agony of the poet.

The day is clear, virginal, sparkling. He asks if it will have the capacity to release him from the sterility he is experiencing; beneath the frozen lake, the reflection of the glacier is visible (the ideal of his unrealized flight).
A swan recalls the pure beauty of the celestial region from where he has descended, the time when he was chaste, innocent

and magnificent, but now he loses all hope because during the sterile winters of "ennui," he failed to sing of those celestial regions. He attempts to shake off the gravity of this agony of impotence. However, although a creature from "beyond," he is now trapped in space.

Perhaps it was his very purity which relegated him to this frozen site where scorn has paralyzed him, destining him to this useless exile.

The metaphor is an image of the poet, asking if this splendid day will perhaps free him from his bout with impotence, wherein he nevertheless has not lost his vision of the unattainable Ideal. He recalls that once he created with pride and joy, yet during his sterile periods, he did not remain true to the Ideal he pursued. Unable now to free himself from this bondage, he is trapped here-below; yet, like the swan, he knows that it is "beyond" where true reality exists.

He feels now like a phantom, and recognizes that his very purity is the cause of his present banishment, and because of that, he has become an object of scorn which he wears like a cloak in his "futile exile."

In a certain sense, the Hamlet symbol is implied—the hero whose will is lamed, and who therefore is immobilized in spite of his awareness of that realm where he longs to be.

Victoriously having renounced glorious suicide....

Victorieusement fui le suicide beau.... Avingnon: 1868 Paris: 1885

This sonnet is addressed to Méry Laurent. Although dealing with a contemplated suicide, a certain lightness of tone prevails, as if from the very start the suicide never really was intended.

The sky is aglow with a splendid crimson and golden sunset. The poet muses at the jest it would be if that sky were the preparation yonder for his burial, and, since he had renounced death, illumined only his absent tomb.

Night falls. Midnight! The colors have faded. Darkness reigns. Yet, as he contemplates Méry, whose head is resting on a pillow, he muses upon her hair which seems to exude its own inner radiance, as if retaining some of the gold of the recent sky braided within it.

Now he compares her to a child empress of an allegory—her hair appearing like a warrior-helmet from which her body, like a stream of roses, pours forth.

Its pure nails offering very high their onyx....

Ses purs ongles très haut dédiant leur onyx.... Paris: 1877

The poet is in a room wherein a baroque candelabra supports the lights. His anguish is personified in the figure offering its onyx on high. His many dreams of creation and glory have not materialized. Like the Phoenix on fire, his inspiration has been consumed, but not gathered up into words (the funeral urn holding the ashes of the Phoenix from which a new flame will rise).

The poem is the dead image of the real experience. Only emptiness is here. Not even the ornate shells which decorated the console table are present, for the Master of the house (the poet) has gone to mourn at the river of death (the Styx), taking with him the empty yet sonorous shell.

Suddenly, through the open window, he beholds in the sky a golden reflection which, in his imagination, assumes the likeness of a unicorn hurling fire at a dying water-nymph. The scene is reflected in a nearby mirror. A comparison with the poem is implied, for the poem is also a kind of mirrored reflection (lifeless) of a greater reality. Yet, it is captured within a structure like the mirrored image is, defined within a frame. Even as the stars in the Constellation of the Seven Sisters (a significant constellation in esoterica) are defined for earth cognition in the mirror, so the poem captures and transmits experience of the Spirit to cognition.

The verbal texture of the above poem is noteworthy, and the very sound structure imaginatively reveals the complex process of cognition in fifteen lines of poetry. Time and again, but here in particular, a reader may deduce Mallarmé's familiarity with the philosophy of such thinkers of his time as Hegel.

Sonnet

(For your dear dead lady, her friend)

Sonnet (Pour votre chère morte, son ami) Paris: 1877

The man is seated at midnight in a room alone, near a hearth of dying embers, murmuring the name of his dead beloved.

The returned spirit of the dead woman speaks, addressing her grieving survivor who is not yet ready to cross the threshold of the sepulchre.

The poem is filled with negatives: the dark sepulchre absent of flowers in this somber winter. He is deaf, she says, to the stroke of midnight (an ending and a beginning)—a midnight, the "vain" number twelve—and he stays awake, imagining the phantom of the dead seated in the easy-chair.

Should he wish to re-experience this "visitation," she says, he must not place heavy bouquets on the sepulchre. Visitation has a double meaning. To experience the supersensible, there must be absence, purity ("too many flowers"—a rich experience of the senses). She still trembles to be with him, and it is enough to hear him murmur her name.

The Tomb of Edgar Poe

Le Tombeau d'Edgar Poe Paris: 1876

Edgar Poe died in 1849, but it was not until 1875 that a monument was erected to him in Baltimore.

This sonnet, wrote Mallarmé, was recited at the unveiling of a "block of basalt as a monument to Poe, with which America weighted down the poet's light shadow, words to make sure that it never reappeared."

The sonnet is a passionate cry of indignation against the treatment Poe received when alive—abuse, rejection, with which he, Mallarmé, identified.

First quatrain:

Now that Poe is dead, his essence, which will live into eternity, rises and defines him as genius.

He is like the Archangel Mich-a-el—the cosmic intelligence—who slew, with his Iron sword, the Dragons of evil (Hydra).

Second quatrain:

Just as the Hydra emitted "vile spasms" when the Archangel wished to purify the earth, so Poe, as the Angel whose work purified and raised the language of humanity, brought forth accusations of black magic and alcoholism. "They" refers to the vile crowd.

First tercet:

The block erected at Baltimore had no carved bas-relief. Mallarmé exclaims "O lament" if we cannot fill that lack. Through the Poem, the bas-relief can be drawn from the hostile earth and sky, and so "adorn the shining tomb of Poe." (His tomb is like a star, shining.)

Second tercet:

The tomb of black basalt is a meteorite, an aerolith (containing purifying iron) fallen from the sky in some "dim disaster" to purify the earth. May this stone (and poem) at least prevent future abuses ("blasphemies") against the poet.

The Tomb of Charles Baudelaire

Le Tombeau de Charles Baudelaire   Paris: 1893

Mallarmé was chosen to be head of a committee to erect a monument to Baudelaire and to edit a volume of works by various writers in dedication.

First quatrain:

The setting is a cemetery where the open grave of Baudelaire is visible, revealing the pipes beneath surrounded by mud and ooze. These pipes in France are often referred to as "The Temple," and Mallarmé uses that to create multiple meaning by evoking an Egyptian tomb. In the lamplight, the reflection creates an image of mud with rubies emerging from the drooling ooze. The orifice is agape and, in the metaphor, becomes the open mouth in a ferocious howl of Anubis, the Egyptian dog-headed god who leads the dead beyond the threshold.

Second quatrain:

The smoking gas twists the wick of the streetlamp, causing the flame to rise in spite of it. It is like one who effaces abuses suffered by Baudelaire during his lifetime, when he was castigated by critics and colleagues. In the lamplight, the flame symbolizing the poetry of Baudelaire has the shape of a pubis, symbol of creative fertility. Also, it is like a wing about to take flight.

First and second tercets:

The dead leaves of the wreath symbolize banal comments which cannot rightly evaluate Baudelaire's achievement. However, his veiled etheric Shade is present, shielding, protecting him, and embodying that aspect of his work which at times seems venomous, yet in reality makes one aware of another vision of truth and beauty.

Tomb
(of Verlaine)

Tombeau (de Verlaine) Paris: 1897

The "pious hands," representing the conventional righteous of the time (perhaps the Catholic Church), maligned Verlaine for his frank unconventional behavior which they rigidly equated with original sin. They will not succeed in destroying him nor his precious contribution to humanity. In a more enlightened time, all will be otherwise.

The monotonous cooing of the ringdove recalls the somber mourning without sincerity, while the dark clouds (which resemble sepulchres and conceal the "full-blown" star—Verlaine's works) recall the sufferings of Verlaine. In the future that star will pour light upon humanity.

The true Verlaine is not to be found in the externals of his life. He is eternal now among the grasses, meeting death in tranquility. In fact, he has not really died. He himself now recognizes that as he was maligned, death itself has been maligned. It is not a deep dark river wherein all disappears forever, but a shallow stream which will not extinguish the light of his achievement, and this will continue to enrich the future.

Tribute
(to Richard Wagner)

Hommage (à Richard Wagner) Paris: 1885

First quatrain:

The old elegance of Theatre ("moire") is dying, and memory of the public is short. That process will be hastened by the death of Wagner, its principal pillar.

Second quatrain:

The heroic poetry of the past, which thrilled the reader and no longer is a winged song soaring above the banal, now is to be placed on dusty shelves ("rather bury it deep in a closet").

First tercet:

Although when his work was first performed, it was hated by audiences and attacked by critics ("the mocking original fracas"), Wagner now rays forth transcendent light from the new temple. He has emerged as a great hero among the geniuses ("those of masterly brilliance") onto the outer sanctuary of the temple created for them.

Second tercet:

The sound of triumphant golden trumpets announces Richard Wagner as a godly hero of the new Mysteries, consecrating a new art which may be appreciated, even on the written page.

Tribute
(to Puvis de Chavannes)

Hommage (à Puvis de Chavannes) Paris: 1895

The artist is like a shepherd who has beaten his fists in vain against the Azure, yet who continues to persist in making a new vision gush forth through his art.

Thus, Puvis de Chavannes, avant garde, lived as a solitary (yet never alone) to lead his century to drink at the spring, or to reveal Aphrodite, the Goddess of Beauty who never dies, and whom his genius unveils ("the nymph without a shroud").

His vision encompassed the future beyond his age—as one who taps for water along the future, he uncovers a new spring, and his foot leads to the place where he will strike to make the spring emerge.

To the sole concern of voyaging....

Au seul souci de voyager.... Paris: 1898

This sonnet is addressed to one who would voyage beyond the material earth to a purer realm, which Mallarmé calls the "cape" which the ship rounds. It is the artist who guides the ship, about which a bird of annunciation frolics (perhaps like the Raven of Edgar Poe), crying of night, despair and precious gems, but the cry is in vain, for the helm does not veer off its course. The artist and Vasco de Gamma are associated with the immortal. In spite of the obstacles and the lure of "precious gems," Vasco (or the Poet) sails on to unknown lands.

The symbol of the voyage is always the quest of the artist.

The whole soul enfurled....

Toute l'âme résumée....   Paris: 1895

This is an Elizabethan sonnet.

In "Divagations," Mallarmé wrote, "I unite this meditation with the smoke of my cigar so as to be able to follow them both, satisfied, diminishing together, before sitting down to a poem, where it will reappear, perhaps, veiled...."

The poem is like a whiff of smoke breathed forth from a cigar when one inhales and exhales, and which proves the existence of a lighted cigar. Thus, the poem also attests to the poet-creator. The poem appears and vanishes as in smoke rings. One must not include the "real" which is static and too precise. The ashes of the "real" must be shaken off so that the core of fire may glow.

To smoke a cigar properly requires a certain skill. So does the writing of a poem, which cannot be written hastily, but slowly as a meditation, so that the core transcends the "ash" of the "real," bringing about a transformation into the imaginative.

Does all Pride turn to smoke at evening....

Tout Orgueil fume-t-il du soir....   Paris: January 1887

First quatrain:
    At the evening of one's life, all glory, recognition, pride, which briefly bestowed an illusion of immortality, are extinguished.

Second quatrain:
    Once, the poet ("the Heir") received recognition, but it can no longer be salvaged (fallen trophies). Even were he to reappear upon the literary scene, he would go unrecognized.

First tercet:
    At this sepulchre of rejection, the agonies of the past return.

Second tercet:

The console table (the instrument where he produced his poetry), however, remains. Upon its surface a flare is reflected, which, though isolated and beneath a tombstone (the marble), still bears light. The implication is that although now neglected, that small flame (the creative deed) is in the world, bringing hope that someday it will be re-ignited.

Risen from the croup and the leap....

Surgi de la croupe et du bond.... Paris: January 1887

First quatrain:

The stem rises within the glass vase, but, through neglect, it never flowers. This may symbolize the act of creation which is begun, but as a result of neglect, the work is not fulfilled. This may also refer to a love one bears another which is aborted by neglect.

Second quatrain:

As two never feel the same passion at the same time, so the poet, like a painted "sylph" on a ceiling, is unable to coalesce with his muse—or is unable to bring forth a poem filled with feeling and imagination.

First tercet:

The vase, empty of fecundating fluid, is like a widow who will not consent to the act of passion which would give birth to the "flower" (the child; the poem)—a light out of the darkness.

Second tercet:

There may have been an annunciation of a work of art, but it remains dismal and without passion.

A lace curtain is made void....

Une dentelle s'abolit.... Paris: 1887

A lace curtain evokes a mystical bed, no place for a consummation. In other words, no bed is here for the act of creation upon the void. Thus, the divine purpose of existence is denied (a blasphemy). The embrace is only that of two white curtains which fly toward a pallid pane: No conflict which might bring forth a creative act occurs.

But in the soul of the poet, where resides the "golden dream," reposes a "lute," symbol of poetry, shaped like a womb, and therein the poet (musician of the Void—of the Spirit) may create by bringing forth the imagery of his intuition. Therefore, he has no need of a bed, but is able to transcend the physical and give birth to the Higher self ("as Son")—the *I am*, through giving birth to the Verb (the Word—the Logos).

The lace curtain of the mystical bed becomes the esoteric veil beyond which lies the supersensible, the Eternal, and that may be revealed by the Poet.

Banal reality is destroyed. The curtains vanish to reveal a spiritual metamorphosis.

What silk in the balms of time....

Quelle soie aux baumes de temps.... Paris: 1881

This sonnet is one of the triptych: "Tout orgeuil," "Surgi de la croupe" and "Quelle soie."

Once again, we are dealing with "Hair," which here becomes silken flags.

The "silk embalmed by time" represents flags, symbols of collective glory which time has dulled and deadened. The "Chimera," or poetic Ideal, has become a ghost.

Perhaps a parade was passing outside with frayed flags flying. Here within sits Méry at her mirror, combing her hair which is like a golden cloud. This image is like a bridge from reality to the Ideal. The poet will forget his frustrated longings for glory if he might but bury a kiss in her hair.

Note the brilliant sound structure; the rhymes: *temps, tends, méditants, content, amant.* The verbal texture is brilliant—Mallarmé at his best.

To bring myself into your story....

M'introduire dans ton histoire.... Paris: 1885

This sonnet probably was addressed to Méry Laurent.
Once again, it is the timid poet addressing an ideal woman.
He is like a hero in a fairy story wherein the hero must undergo trials in order to obtain the hand of the Fairy Princess.
Although he has striven to "ravish glaciers," that is, the most difficult realms (as poet), he hesitates to conquer her for fear of rejection.
Nevertheless, his feelings for her have filled him with renewed energy and creativity, as when fireworks soar and explode in the sky, bursting into jewels of color, and although they are illusory and evanescent, they make it possible for him to distinguish the wheel of his creativity as a vesperal prayer.
Some critics have interpreted the title as being erotic, and the phrase "ton histoire" does have such a nuance in French. It also may signify her destiny, her history.
Those who have experienced a display of fireworks in France have witnessed among them depictions of flaming chariots in the sky.

Silenced by the oppressive cloud....

A la nue accablante tu.... Paris: 1895

This sonnet inevitably makes us think of "A Throw of the Dice" ("Un Coup De Dés").
There is the hovering possibility of shipwreck, and the actual wreck. The Master's previous dynamism and assurance

have given way to the slavish wails and cries of the heirs, and the ship formerly so noble has been torn apart by the tempest and swallowed up by the sea (in which all reality is dissolved). The white foam is the only attestation to the ensuing dematerialization and the child-siren was the beginning of art's realization, inevitably destroyed by "the fatal law" of the death sentence which awaits all humans and all endeavors. The "so-white hair" has a multiple nuance of age and death which, without compassion, destroy youthful enthusiasm and creativity.

The "oppressive cloud" is the hovering of that disaster.

The trumpet, usually an instrument of an annunciation, has been drowned out by the tempest of inevitable destruction, as have been the cries of the shipwrecked sailors. Only the foam, symbol of some pure essence, remains as witness to the wreck—the foundering of all creative dreams and efforts. The abyss, wherein are the great forces of darkness, seems in a fury that the perdition was not even more destructive. The basalt and lava cliff and the black cloud are familiar to us from the "Tombeau" poems.

On a more individual level, the poem could imaginatively represent a terrible rejection of the poet by the Philistine uncomprehending of his time, when even his poet-colleagues were too slavish to defend lofty poetry. The critics, perhaps, were not content merely to express an negative opinion, but were wildly abusive, as those with rigidified conventional ideas and prejudices become when faced with the new, and to them, the incomprehensible. Such rejection only serves to destroy the emerging new, truly Ideal, revelation.

Having closed my books....

Mes bouquins refermés.... Paris: 1887

Seated by the hearth which should symbolize the love between him and his wife, who is in another room, the poet has been reading about Ancient Greece. The cold silent winter outside the window with its snow-drifts sweeping across the bare land cannot compare to the landscape of his imagination—an ancient scene where hyacinths grow and the ocean beats against the shore. In contrast, the present brings only "ennui." True "reality" lies in the past, in "Absence." The present love of woman cannot compare to that of his dream—some ancient Amazon with a seared breast who excites his ardor more than any actual present human love is capable of doing.

Paphos, incidentally, is the site of the Ancient Mysteries of Aphrodite.

Toast

Salut Paris: 1893

In his Bibliography of 1898, Mallarmé writes, "Toast—this sonnet, in proposing a toast recently at a dinner of *La Plume*, at which I had the honor to preside...."

First quatrain:
The poet raises his cup in a toast and speaks: This poem is only a bit of foam, like the champagne in my raised cup. The verse can designate it as the whiteness outlines the cup. It evokes the sea where a troupe of sirens is plunging upside down.
This recalls to the reader the upside-down siren of "Un Coup De Dés" ("A Throw of the Dice"), and the Naiads who "fled or plunged" in "Afternoon of a Faun." In other words, it evokes that realm of Spirit and creativity beyond the here and now.

Second quatrain:
He addresses the assembled poets: The life of a poet is like a quest by sea where the poet sets forth courageously to face the upcoming trials ("the tide of thunderbolts and winters").

First tercet:
He is intoxicated, yet "fearless of the pitching," and remains "upright" in offering this toast. Intoxication here has a double meaning. It is a bit of humor connected with the champagne, but also a symbol indicating an exhilarated state of creativity.

Second tercet:
The concerns and symbols of the true poet are "solitude, reef,

star": The poet is a solitary, an individual whose spiritual quest rises from within. The reef is the symbol of the rock on which Hamlet, symbol of the poet, stands facing the abyss which he must conquer. "Star" is that divine constellation which has designated the Poet to be the spokesman of the Ideal, and toward which he strives to reascend. The "white concern of our sail" is the paper on which the poet creates the poem, to be conquered by the "plume," the pen.

This was one of the last poems which Mallarmé composed. Although a short poem, it contains some of the major symbols of Mallarmé, all of which were included in his masterpiece, "Un Coup De Dés."

A THROW OF THE DICE WILL NEVER ABOLISH CHANCE

UN COUP DE DÉS JAMAIS N'ABOLIRA LE HASARD Paris: 1897

"Un Coup De Dés" was first published in the magazine *Cosmopolis* in 1897, and in book form by Gallimard a short time later. The version printed here follows the Gallimard edition which Mallarmé designed before his death. Mallarmé indicated that the poem is to be read lengthwise, starting at the left side of the page, moving across the fold of the book to the edge of the opposite page.

Each page of the poem forms an ideogram—an image of whiteness of sky and ocean, storm waves, crests and troughs, male and female, wing and bird, sail and boat, the Dipper or Septentrion, etc.

The four themes, introduced by the title, according to Mallarmé, are equivalent to the four phrase movement of a symphony. That number, representing many phases of life and time—four divisions of a day, four seasons, four stages of total time, etc. is an important part of the pattern which unifies the poem.

UN COUP DE DÉS
JAMAIS
N'ABOLIRA
LE HASARD

in large, bold, Roman caps, is the first and major theme, each word group forming the central idea of the four divisions of the work. The secondary theme, in small caps, may be traced through the poem:

"EVEN WHEN CAST IN ETERNAL CIRCUMSTANCES/ AT THE HEART OF A SHIPWRECK/ WHETHER/ THE MASTER/ EVEN IF IT EXISTED/ EVEN IF IT BEGAN AND EVEN IF IT CEASED/ EVEN IF SUMMED UP/ EVEN IF IT ENLIGHTENED/ NOTHING/ WILL HAVE TAKEN PLACE/ BUT THE PLACE/ EXCEPT/ PERHAPS/ A CONSTELLATION."

The words in lower case carry out other ideas, and an adjacent theme is carried by those in upper and lower case:

Abyss/ Number/ Spirit/ Betrothal.

The seven point type, the italics, all form individual counterpoints.

The central idea is that "Thought" or the creative act, "A Throw of the Dice" (UN COUP DE DÉS), will never (JAMAIS) abolish (N'ABOLIRA) Death, the Absolute, Chance (LE HASARD). This is the opposite of the theme expressed in *Igitur*: Man through a supreme act, (Art), can conquer *le hasard*.

The Boatswain, the Master, the Artist, the Poet, Creative Man, (LE MAÎTRE), stands at the helm of his foundering ship, (Life, energy, all the creative forces over which he once held control, which now he has lost [jadis il empoignait la barre] in a tornado which is pulling him into the whirlpool [L'Abîme, le gouffre]). Driven wild by the indifferent neutrality of the abyss (la neutralité identique du gouffre), he hesitates to make the last throw of the dice which he holds in his clenched fist, which might save the ship (himself); finally realizing that nothing (Rien), not even the "unique number" (the great work of art, the supreme act), can save him from the anonymity of Death (the Absolute, perdition, the final "Hasard," the void) in which all reality is dissolved (en quoi toute réalité se dissout).

Yet, a point of light saves the poem from complete darkness. Perhaps (PEUT-ÊTRE), in the altitude, beyond human comprehension and perception, there is a last single, dying constellation which retains a point of consciousness which reflects onto the void where he tried to conquer oblivion.

Aldan Reads Mallarmé

Daisy Aldan reads 18 selections from
To Purify the Words of the Tribe

Cassette — $11.95
Shipping — $1.25 domestic $3.00 overseas

Send check or money order to:

Sky Blue Press
13149 Balfour
Huntington Woods, MI 48070 USA

For more information, e-mail skybluepr@aol.com
or call 248-544-0546